D0566864

Public Education

Gerald Leinwand, Ph.D.

Produced by the Philip Lief Group, Inc.

Facts On File

New York • Oxford

To my teacher,
Theodore Brameld,
distinguished philosopher
of American education

Public Education (American Issues Series)

Copyright © 1992 by Gerald Leinwand and The Philip Lief Group

Facts On File, Inc.   Facts On File Limited
460 Park Avenue South   c/o Roundhouse Publishing Ltd.
New York NY 10016   P. O. Box 140
USA   Oxford OX2 75F
                                    United Kingdom

Library of Congress Cataloging-in-Publication Data
Leinwand, Gerald
    Public education / Gerald Leinwand.
        p. cm. — (American Issues)
    "Produced by the Philip Lief Group, Inc."
    Includes bibliographical references and index.
    Summary: Examines the history, problems, and concerns of public
education in America.
    ISBN 0-8160-2100-7
    1. Public schools—United States—History. 2. Education—United
States—Aims and objectives. 3. Educational sociology—United
States. [1. Education. 2. Schools.] I. Title. II. Series:
American issues (New York, N.Y.)
LA217.2.L45   1992
371'.01'0973—dc20   91-39721

A British CIP catalogue record for this book is available from the British Library.

Facts On File books are available at special discounts when purchased in
bulk quantities for businesses, associations, institutions or sales promotions.
Please contact our Special Sales Department in New York at 212/683-2244
(dial 800/322-8755 except in NY, AK or HI) or in Oxford at 865/728399.

Jacket design by Catherine Hyman
Composition by Facts On File, Inc.
Manufactured by The Maple-Vail Book Manufacturing Group
Printed in The United States of America

10 9 8 7 6 5 4 3 2 1

This book is printed on acid-free paper.

943566

C O N T E N T S

Preface   iv

1 A Priority for the Twenty-first Century   1

2 A Nation's Schools   15

3 The Achievements of the Nation's Schools   32

4 Who Should Be Taught?   47

5 What Should Be Taught?   73

6 Who Should Teach?   100

7 An Agenda for the Twenty-first Century   123

Bibliography   134

Index   137

P R E F A C E

Myth and nostalgia hang like smog over American education and impair our vision as to how to retain the best values of the common school while making them responsive to the needs of the 21st century. The myth is that schools were somehow better in earlier generations than they are today. The truth is that each generation has expressed dissatisfaction with its schools and sought to improve them. The nostalgia reflects our respect for those heros of folklore who, with little formal schooling, rose to success through their own diligence, honesty and common sense.

Because we long for a time that never was, and cannot establish a consensus about the shape of the years ahead, myth and nostalgia cloud our thinking about the kind of public schools we ought to have. Yet, in thinking about schools for tomorrow, we can no longer swagger through the 21st century by thumbing our noses at formal education. "Street smarts" will always be a necessary condition for survival but will never be a sufficient condition for sustained national competitiveness or effective leadership on the world's stage.

In this volume, as in others in the American Issues series, a problem is explored and questioned. In this case, we survey the triumph and tragedy of America's public schools. We hope the book will encourage Americans to think about the kind of schools they ought to have and to heed the warning of the British philosopher Alfred North Whitehead: "The nation that does not value trained intelligence is doomed."

Gerald Leinwand
New York, New York

A Priority for the Twenty-first Century

Perhaps no other institution in American society— from defense to big business to medicine—is understood to be as vital to the country's future as the American school. In America, education is often associated with everything that is right or wrong about society, from literacy to illiteracy, to minority group achievement and racial prejudice, to patriotism and civil unrest. There are probably as many opinions about America's educational system as there are Americans. And on this most would agree: We expect much from our schools, and the schools are not perfect.

Beginning with his 1988 presidential campaign, when he outlined his education initiative—America 2000—President Bush made it clear that he viewed the American educational system as inadequate and in need of serious reform. Though not always agreeing with his approach, many Americans were eager to join with him in criticizing the educational system.

In the summer of 1990, at a meeting of the American Federation of Teachers, Albert Shanker, its president, had this to say about the current state of American education: "How bad are things? Ninety-five percent of the kids who go to college in the U.S. would not be admitted to college anywhere else in the world." Mr. Shanker challenged his audience to test their own 17-year-olds by having them explain a newspaper editorial, write something or do a two-part math problem.[1] What is noteworthy about his statement is that even among educators, who are ordinarily supportive of their schools and champions of their profession, the problems of American public schools during the last decade of the 20th century are being acknowledged. During the 1980s, the state of public education in America was the subject of front-page newspaper headlines, feature magazine articles and countless television programs. These popular, and often dramatic, accounts of the shortcomings in the nation's schools were based on a series of alarming reports of studies conducted by distinguished educators. Their conclusion: American education needs improvement.

Let's take a closer look at these problems.

A Nation at Risk

In the report of the National Commission on Excellence in Education titled *A Nation at Risk* (1983), the investigators wrote:

... While we can take justifiable pride in what our schools and colleges have historically accomplished and contributed to the United States and the well-being of its people, the educational foundations of our society are presently being eroded by a rising tide of mediocrity that threatens our very future as a nation and a people. What was unimaginable a generation ago has begun to occur—others are matching and surpassing our educational attainments.

If an unfriendly foreign power had attempted to impose on America the mediocre educational performance that exists today, we might well have viewed it as an act of war. As it stands we have allowed this to happen to ourselves.[2]

The realities of the current state of America's public schools and their students continue to disturb the American people:

- Every eight seconds of the school day, an American child drops out of school (552,000 in the 1987–88 school year).
- Every school day, an estimated 135,000 American children bring guns to school.
- Among six industrialized countries (France, England, Wales, Canada, the Netherlands and the United States), the United States had the highest teen pregnancy rate.
- American school children know less geography than school children in Iran, less math than school children in Japan and less science than school children in Spain.
- The United States makes a proportionately smaller investment in education than the five other industrialized nations mentioned above.
- American students' test scores are lower than those of students in Japan, Hungary, England and other countries.
- Between 1979 and 1986, federal assistance in education dropped 22.4%.[3]
- In other countries, young men and women of about high school age spend more days in school than those in the United States. While American students spend about 180 days in school, pupils in Japan attend for 243 days, those in the Soviet Union attend for 208, Hong Kong pupils spend 195 days in school, and British and Canadians spend 192 and 186, respectively.[4]
- Seventy-three percent of American 13-year-olds watch television three or more hours a day. The number of children who watch TV for a similar amount of time in other countries: Britain, 72%; Canada, 65%; Ireland, 55%; Spain, 54%; and South Korea, 51%.[5]
- Only 27% of American students spend two or more hours a day on homework. Compare the percentage of 13-year-

olds who spend two or more hours a day on homework in some other countries: Spain, 59%; Ireland, 57%; Britain, 35%; South Korea, 28%; and English-speaking Canada, 25%.[6]

Will America's youth be educated enough to serve themselves and their country in the next century? When more than half of the new jobs will require education beyond high school, how will the next generation compete? It is no exaggeration to say that the future of the nation rests upon the answers to these questions.

A Golden Age?

Because of America's high expectations, it is easier to blame the public schools for society's shortcomings than to praise the schools for their achievements. Among the reasons for this negative attitude is that educators themselves have overstated the schools' benefits to society. In seeking support, educators promised that public schools could make youth literate, workers more efficient and, as a result, make industry more profitable. Crime would be substantially reduced; health would improve as children learned the rudiments of personal hygiene and community health; immigrants would be absorbed, learn English and rapidly assimilate into the American culture, so as not be a burden to society. Publicly supported schools would provide a means of upward mobility and contribute to the end of poverty.

Schools indeed went a long way toward helping to alleviate some of these problems, and there is a tendency to view the past as a "golden age." When we probe, however, for a "golden age" of American education, we find this era difficult to identify. What years were really golden when compared to the others? What made them so golden? For one thing, in the past there were smaller numbers of children and youth attending school.

Those who went to school for any length of time tended to be intellectually and/or economically privileged. Most students who were not of a privileged background left school early, even though universal education was set forth as a goal in the United States.

Current judgments of school success or failure are made on the basis of a host of statistical data not available until relatively recently. Would Americans take a favorable view of their schools during the "golden age" had statistics about achievement levels in reading, arithmetic, writing or dropout rates existed 75 years ago? Prior to World War I, whatever success was attributed to the public schools was done so on the basis of intuition or perception rather than statistical measurement of educational accomplishment.

In other words, we can really only guess at how "good" the educational system was of even the most recent past. Our knowledge is grounded on opinions and guesses, and, over the years, memories and recollections become less and less reliable.

Each generation has had its educational critics. As you will see in the chapters that follow, some were hostile to the notion of popular education altogether. Others complained of declining standards. For example, in 1874, high school teachers complained; "It is [our] opinion . . . that from one-fourth to one-half of the pupils are not greatly benefited by their course of study. These students lack interest, industry, effort and purpose, and are too feebly endowed mentally. . . ."[7]

In 1894, a Committee of Ten on Secondary Studies, appointed by the National Education Association, convened to propose a revised high school curriculum. They concluded that "only a small proportion of all the children in the country . . . show themselves able to profit by an education prolonged to the eighteenth year."[8] Although aware that many students were failing, the committee went on to propose a highly traditional study of the academic disciplines for all students.

A few years later, complaining of "the menace of present educational methods," one writer declared: "The mental nourishment we spoon-feed our children is not only minced but peptonized so that their brains digest it without effort and without benefit and the result is the anaemic intelligence of the average American schoolchild."[9] A British observer of American schools found the curriculum contained "too much candy and ice cream" and an inadequate amount of "oatmeal porridge."[10]

In 1909, a systematic study was attempted to find out why children drop out of school. The conclusion is as valid today as it was then. Children drop out of school because they are failing. Lack of success was and remains the most common reason for leaving school prematurely. By this measure, it was concluded that the elementary schools of the earlier 20th century were failing the children and were in urgent need of reform; if children felt they were achieving some success by being in school, they would stay.[11]

Between 1911 and 1913, in its *Final Report*, the Committee on School Inquiry startled the nation by reporting that "illiteracy in the United States is fifty times greater than that of Germany, Norway, Sweden or Denmark."[12] In fact, during World War I, the military turned away thousands of potential soldiers because they were illiterate.

During the years after World War I, the following complaints were heard about the public schools:

- In 1929, educators were worried about the "large number of pupils playing hookey."
- In 1938, the Regents of New York State reported that in their state, "the boys and girls who leave high school without graduating outnumber the graduates nearly two to one."
- The public became ever more aware of reading problems

during the early 1940s as the nation sought to induct draftees for military service in World War II. About 200,000 men were barred because of illiteracy.

- In February 1947, Benjamin Fine, education editor for the *New York Times*, wrote a series of articles demonstrating what he called the American public school system's "most serious crisis in history." In a six-month investigation of the nation's schools, he reported that since 1940, 350,000 teachers left the schools to serve in military or civilian capacities in World War II. One in every seven remaining teachers had a substandard, emergency, teaching certificate. There were 125,000 new and inexperienced teachers. About 60,000 teachers had only a high school education; 6,000 schools closed because of a shortage of teachers. The average teacher's salary of $37 per week was lower than that of the average truck driver, garbage collector or bartender.

Gross inequities existed. In some classroom units as much as $6,000 was spent per unit while others spent as little as $100. School buildings stood in deplorable condition while both the Soviet Union and Great Britain spent more of their national income on schools.

- In 1955, Rudolf Flesch's book *Why Johnny Can't Read* became a best-seller as more Americans began to fear their children were not reading as well as they should. Parents felt that America's teaching methods were faulty.
- In 1957, the Soviet satellite *Sputnik* was launched into space, giving the Soviets a head start over the United States in the race to conquer space. Americans worried about falling behind in science and technology, areas in which the nation felt a great deal of pride in accomplishment. As a consequence, the merits of the American school system

were called into serious question.

- In the late 1950s, a journalist for the *World Telegram and Sun* took a teaching job in a New York City junior high school. From this vantage point, he reported on the assaults, brawls, disruptions and violence rampant in the schools.
- In 1958, the *New York Times* reported nearly 40,000 pupils were left back that year, most often for reading problems, and some because of "general neglect of studies, especially in math."
- In 1961, the superintendent of New York City schools announced one-third of all junior high school students were more than two years behind in reading, and 10,000 seventh-graders were reading four years below level.[13]

Although this historic overview places current problems in context, they are no less daunting: As the 20th century draws to a close, illiteracy is a growing problem. A new term, "innumeracy," has been coined to draw attention to a national deficiency in the mastery of basic skills in mathematics. There is increased concern that our current system of education is not giving its students the tools they need to compete successfully in the new global marketplace. Can the schools be fixed? If so, how? By whom? If more money is needed, who pays? If schools cannot be fixed, what should replace them?

The purpose of this book is to try to get at the answers to these and other questions about the public schools. By being informed about their history, and their strengths and weaknesses, you will be in a better position to help improve them.

A Lost Generation

In his 1978 book, *The Literary Hoax: The Decline of Reading, Writing, and Learning in the Public Schools and What We Can Do About It*, Paul Copperman wrote: "Each generation has outstripped its parents in education, in literacy, and in economic attainment. For the first time in the history of our country, the educational skills of one generation will not surpass, will not equal, will not even approach, those of their parents."[14] He was quoted with the approval of the authors of *A Nation at Risk*. This government report went on to identify areas in public education that need substantial improvement. While this report was one of many that were generally critical of the schools, it seemed particularly disturbing because of its harsh language, and carried the serious weight of sponsorship by Terrell Bell when he was secretary of the U.S. Department of Education.

Some educators view today's students as an educationally "lost" generation. Their position comes from the following criticisms of the nation's schools:

- International comparisons of student achievement reveal that on tests of 19 academic subjects, American students were never first or second. In fact, in comparison with other industrialized nations, the United States scored last seven times.

- About 23 million American adults are functionally illiterate by the simplest tests of everyday reading, writing and comprehension.

- About 13% of all 17-year-olds in the United States can be considered functionally illiterate. Functional illiteracy among minority youth may run as high as 40%. People who are functionally illiterate may be able to read and write their own names and addresses, but be unable to function in society because they cannot read the directions on a voting machine, understand a subway map, figure exact change, comprehend more than headlines in a daily local newspaper or calculate simple measurements.

- Over half the population of gifted students are not achieving their potential based on their scores on ability tests.

Simply put, too many people are not trying hard enough.
- The College Board's Scholastic Aptitude Test (SAT) demonstrates a virtually unbroken decline from 1963 through the 1980s. Average verbal scores fell more than 50 points and average math scores dropped nearly 40 points. Of course, a wider range of students now take the SAT than in previous decades. Still, the decline is alarming.
- Many 17-year-olds do not possess the "higher order" intellectual skills that should be expected of them. That is, nearly 40% cannot draw inferences from written material; only one-fifth can write a persuasive essay and only one-third can solve a mathematics problem requiring several steps.
- Science and mathematics achievement has steadily declined, and one-quarter of all mathematics courses now taught in public four-year colleges are remedial in nature. This is despite the recurrent fear that we are losing ground to foreign nations in these vital subjects.
- Businesses and the military complain about the millions of dollars they spend on costly remedial education and training programs in basic skills such as reading, writing, spelling and computation.
- Secondary school curricula have been diluted so that they no longer have a central purpose. In a "cafeteria"-style curriculum, students choose the "desserts" and "appetizers" and shun the main (hard) courses.
- In 1980, only eight states required high schools to offer foreign language instruction, and none required students to take the course.[15]

Many other reports followed, each with a special emphasis, yet each also confirmed the findings of *A Nation at Risk*. A 1983 report of the Twentieth-Century Fund, titled *Making the Grade*, declared: "By almost every measure—the commitment and competency of teachers, student test scores, truancy and dropout rates, crimes of violence—the performance of our schools falls far short of expectations."[16]

The report of the National Science Board, *Educating Americans for the 21st Century*, also published in 1983, was critical of the nation for "failing to provide its own children with the intellectual tools needed for the 21st century. . . . Already the quality of our manufactured products, the viability of our trade, our leadership in research and development, and our standards of living are strongly challenged. Our children could be stragglers in a world of technology. We must not let this happen; America must not become an industrial dinosaur. We must not provide our children a 1960s education for a 21st-century world."[17]

The close relationship of American schooling to American economic competitiveness became the thrust of *Action for Excellence: A Comprehensive Plan to Improve Our Nation's Schools*, the report made in 1983 by the Education Commission of the States. The commission deplored "the absence of clear, compelling and widely agreed-upon goals for improving educational performance."[18]

In *High School: A Report on Secondary Education in America*, published in 1983, Ernest Boyer stressed the need for a basic core curriculum for the secondary school and the addition of community service as an integral component of it. All students would study the subjects most effective in helping them become better educated men and women, including the more difficult subjects. Community service, he believes, could help students understand the adult world and provide insights into national and even global problems. Moreover, these real-life experiences would be helpful to students as they formulate career objectives and develop the skills needed to achieve their ambitions.

In his 1984 book *A Place Called School*, John Goodlad identified the conflicting expectations teachers, parents and administrators have about what should take place in school. Theodore Sizer wrote *Horace's Compromise* in 1984 to illustrate the day-today compromises teachers are forced to make because of too many students, inadequate budgets or counterproductive administrative policies and routines.

It may indeed be said that these are the best and worst of times in American education. They are the best of times: *A Nation at Risk acknowledges: "... the average citizen* is better educated and more knowledgeable than the average citizen of a generation ago—more literate, and exposed to more mathematics, literature, and science."[19]

But these are also the worst of times: As an ever-greater proportion of our children complete high school and college, graduates are not as well educated as they were 25 years ago. As *A Nation at Risk* asserts, the failure of the schools to educate graduates as well as they did a generation or two ago has a negative impact that "... likewise cannot be overstated."[20]

In no country in the world do people look to education to lessen the impact of social ills—hunger, drug addiction, violence, crime, teenage pregnancy, homelessness, poverty, disease—as they do in the United States. Thus, only in America do schools have a dual responsibility: to transmit knowledge and to make people better citizens. All countries are committed to providing their students with knowledge, though each country has its own definition of the kind of knowledge it wishes its young to have. But only Americans have faith that schooling can make men and women more noble, help them develop character, improve their civic competence and reduce crime.

It is these high expectations that the goals of President Bush's America 2000 proposal will strive to meet:

1. By the year 2000, all children in America will start school ready to learn.
2. By the year 2000, the high school graduation rate will increase to at least 90%.

3. By the year 2000, American students will complete grades four, eight and twelve, having demonstrated competency in challenging subject matter including English, mathematics, science, history and geography; and every school in America will ensure that all students learn to use their minds well, so they may be prepared for responsible citizenship, further learning and productive employment in our modern economy.
4. By the year 2000, American students will be first in the world in science and mathematics achievement.
5. By the year 2000, every adult American will be literate and will possess the knowledge and skills necessary to compete in a global economy and exercise the rights and responsibilities of citizenship.
6. By the year 2000, every school in America will be free of drugs and violence and will offer a disciplined environment conducive to learning.

The goals of America 2000 are challenging. To improve the quality of learning, educational policy development and practice will need to change dramatically. The schools will need a complete restructuring, which will require increased funding. The debate over competency testing will need to be resolved. Additionally, the goals of better preparing children to begin school, improving the learning environment and increasing the graduation rate will require addressing social problems outside of the schools, such as poverty and drug abuse. Solutions will not come easily. However, if America is to remain competitive in the global economy, our schools will need to play a major role.

In the context of history, President Bush's America 2000 is a continuation of a dialogue about public education that is re-addressed in each generation. The dialogue can be summarized in three basic questions: Who should be taught?

What should be taught? Who should teach? The following chapters address these questions, beginning with how schools evolved into their current form and structure.

Notes

Citations in the notes are brief. Full citations appear in the bibliography.

CHAPTER ONE

1. *The Wall Street Journal*, August 23, 1990.
2. National Commission on Excellence in Education, 5.
3. National Center for Children in Poverty.
4. *Fortune*, Spring, 1990, 50–51.
5. Ibid.
6. Ibid.
7. Wolfthal, 166.
8. Ibid.
9. D'Aimee, 263.
10. Sadler, 228.
11. Ayers.
12. Wolfthal, 165.
13. Ibid.
14. National Commission on Excellence in Education, 11.
15. National Commission on Excellence in Education, 8–23.
16. Twentieth-Century Fund Task Force on Federal Elementary and Secondary Education Policy, 3.
17. National Science Board Commission on Pre-College Education in Mathematics, Science and Technology.
18. Education Commission of the States, 46.
19. National Commission on Excellence in Education, 11.
20. Ibid.

CHAPTER TWO

A Nation's Schools

Think for a moment about your school. It is responsible for doing much more than teaching basic skills and academic subjects. Your school, for example, may teach students to drive, use computers and work out on the parallel bars. You may learn how to draw and paint, how to compose music or to speak a foreign language.

Your school probably forms the hub of your social network; you most likely make many of your friends at school, in your classes and through extracurricular activities and events. Your school may have a student government, newspaper, yearbook, band or orchestra, perhaps a literary magazine and an almost endless variety of after-school activities from athletic teams to zoology clubs. Outside the United States, few schools in the world attempt to do so much for so many.

To better understand how our education system progressed to this point, let's take a closer look at where it all began.

Schools in Early America

Compared to the schools you attend, schools in early 17th-century America were ramshackle affairs, often informally housed in churches or stores designed primarily for other purposes. Some children were also taught in so-called dame schools. *Dame* was a 17th-century term for a woman of authority; in dame schools, children were taught in their teachers' kitchens.

When instruction was provided in a separate building, these colonial elementary schools were mainly one-room cabins with space for no more than 20 to 30 children ranging in age from three to 16. Often the one-room schoolhouse had only a dirt floor and no windows. Sometimes the room had a pot-bellied stove in the center that gave off a small amount of heat. The colonial schoolhouse, a beloved symbol in American folklore, was not a pleasant place at all. It was extremely cold in winter and oppressively hot in summer.

While there were undoubtedly some outstanding and respected teachers in colonial America, many of them were not very educated themselves. It was not unheard of for elementary schools to have teachers who, although dedicated to their students, could offer little else but basic instruction.

In the absence of desks, chalkboards and other visual aids, memorization was the mainstay of instruction. Children memorized the alphabet and the Lord's Prayer from a "hornbook." The hornbook was not really a book, but rather a sheet of paper attached to a wooden paddle and protected from wear by a thin, transparent layer taken from animal horns. Children were expected to sit upright on their benches and memorize an assigned task quietly while the teacher called upon each pupil in turn to determine whether the assigned task had been accomplished. To enforce memorization, teachers made ready use of the rod—a birch switch. Harsh discipline was the rule because, so it was thought: "Foolishness is bound up in the heart of a child; but the rod of correction shall drive it from him." Through this combination of memorization and physical punishment, education was, in a sense, beaten into each child.

Colonial schools offered no grade-to-grade progression from elementary to high school. Because money to pay for schools was often scarce and because child labor was often needed on the family farm, the amount of time students actually spent in school was inadequate to master even a modest curriculum. In some communities children went to school for no more than 30 days a year, and very few went on to high school. Those who did went to a colonial secondary school called Latin Grammar School, which prepared students for college. As the name indicates, mastery of Latin and Greek was the essential core of the curriculum, since these subjects were required for college.

Made in Massachusetts

Modern American public schools were, it is sometimes said, "made in Massachusetts." Although the Massachusetts Bay Colony did not set out to play a leadership role, some of its traditions and methods were adapted by other colonies. As the country evolved into a republic, these traditions spread across the whole nation.

The Protestant religious traditions of England, Scotland and Holland encouraged a desire for universal education—reading and interpreting the Bible for oneself was essential if a child was to become a pious member of the community. To encourage universal literacy, the colony of Massachusetts Bay adopted the "old Deluder Satan Act" in 1647. This act called upon each township of 50 families to engage a teacher to instruct children in reading and writing. Each township of 100 families was required to pay for a grammar (secondary) school to prepare children for college. The purpose of the law was to thwart the plans of "ye ould deluder Satan, to keepe men from the knowledge of ye Scriptures" and to make sure that "ye learning may not be buried in ye grave of your fathers in ye church and commonwealth."

The law planted the roots of three traditions forming the basis of American public education. These traditions are:[1] the obligation of a community to establish schools;[2] local control of schools;[3] the beginning of the "ladder" system of education, meaning that elementary and high schools were separated. All the New England colonies, except Rhode Island, made similar plans for the schooling of their children. For a time, Rhode Island and the Middle Atlantic and Southern Atlantic colonies relied mainly upon private rather than public support for education. When public schools spread throughout every state of the union, however, it was the Massachusetts model that was mainly adopted.

Thus, the concept of public support for education was born.

Forerunners of the Common School

The public school you can now attend, free of charge, was first called the common school. It was "common" because all the children from the community were to enroll irrespective of wealth, social standing, religion or sex. (However, as you will read later in this section, the needs of the poor and those from minority groups were not adequately met.) It was America's unique response to the rapid growth of democracy and industry. The common school's formative years were mainly between 1830 and 1860, but Benjamin Franklin (1706–90) and Thomas Jefferson (1743–1826) were among its forerunners.

In a pamphlet Franklin wrote in 1749, titled *Some Proposals Relating to the Education of Youth in Pennsylvania*, he criticized the emphasis on Latin and Greek in the secondary school and the schools' preoccupation with providing the nation's youth with a strict and exclusively classical college education. To replace this system, he urged the establishment of a new institution called the *academy* that would prepare the young for work as well as for college, and which would emphasize English rather than the classical languages. History, science and agriculture were among the subjects he thought should be taught. Eventually, Franklin's ideas were incorporated into a school later called the University of Pennsylvania.

Thomas Jefferson's views on education differed somewhat from Franklin's. In 1779, Jefferson proposed a bill to the Virginia legislature called the *Bill for the More General Diffusion of Knowledge*. This bill urged that every free child in Virginia be given, without charge, three years of elementary schooling in reading, writing, arithmetic and history. It also proposed that the brightest students be granted scholarships for secondary school and the best of them be granted scholarships to college.

Jefferson's ideas were revolutionary because he urged three years of education—free of charge—for all white children no matter their wealth or intellectual ability. (On the other hand, his theories have also been described as elitist: He saw the school as a place where a "natural aristocracy" of talent is identified.) Jefferson had a practical goal behind this idea. The intellectual elite would be encouraged to pursue even higher levels of education; they would become the leaders in the democratic republic then emerging. Although his bill was never adopted by the Virginia legislature, it was Jefferson who recognized a relationship between education and democracy. He said, "If we expect to be ignorant and free in a state of civilization, we expect what never was and never will be."

During the first half of the 19th century, a distinctive American civilization grew rapidly. New states joined the Union. Universal male suffrage—the right of all men to vote—had been achieved. The opportunity to hold elective office was no longer considered the privilege of only the elite. If all men could vote and hold office, they would have to be educated to perform their civic duties intelligently and responsibly. (Of course, it is important to keep in mind that in the 19th century, "all men" meant all white men. The privileges and responsibilities of black men, Asians or Native Americans were not recognized.)

Interest in reform became widespread as men and women sought to improve a rapidly expanding society. Caring for the insane, rehabilitating convicts, improving the lives of women and children, abolishing slavery, imposing temperance (forbidding the use of alcohol), and absorbing the many immigrants, were among the problems the nation struggled with.

The Common School

The common school movement was not national. Instead, each state sought to respond to the changing times in its own way. While the common school movement was not the work of one person, Horace Mann (1796–1850), the first secretary of education in Massachusetts, is perhaps most clearly associated with it. Horace Mann perceived the common school to be "the great equalizer of the condition of men."

The common school was to be "common" in that it was designed for the children of rich and poor parents alike. All children would be taught in a common environment. Students of every social level, nationality and religion would have the opportunity to sit together and to learn from one another. As one speaker expressed it, "I want to see the children of the rich and the poor sit down side by side on equal terms, as members of one family—a great brotherhood—deeming no one distinguished above the rest but the best scholar and the best boy— giving free and natural play for their affections, at a time of life when lasting friendships are often formed, and the worldliness and pride and envy have not yet alienated heart from heart."[1]

Horace Mann and his colleagues were successful in launching the nation on the most ambitious social experiment ever undertaken anywhere—namely, the mass education of Americans. It was an awesome task that no other country of the day attempted. But the experiment was not mounted without a fight, and some echoes of it are still with us. For example, there were those who felt it was unfair to tax everyone to support the education of other people's children. There were others who opposed the common school because, with the First Amendment to the U.S. Constitution separating church and state, religion would no longer be a major focus of education. Some felt only the barest essentials of reading and writing need be taught, and they opposed the upward extension of the common school to the high school.

Yet, out of this struggle, a common, or public, school emerged that had the following recognizable characteristics: The common school was to teach the three Rs, that is, the reading, writing, arithmetic and spelling essential for practical daily living. The common school would teach both morality—so knowledge would be put to proper use—and patriotism—so loyal citizens would be the products of education.

These goals fostered controversies that continue to this day. How should basic skills be taught and which skills are basic? Without a religious dimension, how can moral education succeed? What *is* moral and how does one teach it? How does one teach patriotism if there are differences of opinion about a particular course of action taken by the nation? Is criticism of the nation in the classroom unpatriotic? Which books should be used as textbooks? Should prayers be said? If so, from which religious source? Who should read them and how often? If the school was to be the chief instrument to absorb and "Americanize" the immigrant and to mold the American character, how could this best be accomplished?

The effectiveness of the common schools was mixed. In the absence of compulsory education, many children of the poor did not go to school. Their work was needed in the family business or on the family farm. Sometimes children lacked minimum food and clothing to get to school. It was often only through the combined efforts of parents and children, working together on farms or in small family businesses, that many immigrant families were able to survive their first generation in America. Later generations, a bit more affluent, did take advantage of the common school, but initially the very poor were unable to benefit from what had been so zealously fought for. Although the common school became the means of upward social and economic mobility for the middle classes, the urban and rural poor were still essentially left out. The distinguished historian of American education Lawrence Cremin has pointed out that we have tended to overstate the "commonness" of common schools. [2] As is often the case with programs that are designed to benefit the "masses," the educational system did indeed reach the majority. However, many of the neediest groups slipped through the cracks. The 19th-century founders of the common school were not sensitive to the needs of slaves, urban and rural poor and Native Americans. Consequently, those groups were not helped to an improved education and were thus kept out of the mainstream of economic mobility.

In keeping within the scope of the 19th-century sensibility, in its earliest stages of development the common school was dedicated to educating a substantial portion of the population. The degree to which our education system has succeeded illustrates the conviction behind the effort. However, the needs of American society are constantly changing and growing in complexity. To keep up, our educational system must continue to redefine the goal of education for all, backed up by the additional muscle provided by new devices, techniques and approaches made possible by modern educational research and technology. "What the best and wisest parent wants for his own child," the philosopher John Dewey (1859–1952) declared in 1899 in a series of lectures on *The School and Society*, "that must the community want for all of its children. Any other idea for our schools is narrow and unlively; acted upon, it destroys our democracy." [3]

The key to the continuing success of the American way of education is self-examination, and change, in pursuit of excellence. One of the most historically significant examples of the progress such scrutiny can bring is the 1954 decision of the Supreme Court of the United States in the case of *Brown v. the Board of Education* of Topeka, Kansas. This landmark case struck down the practice of "separate but equal schools." *Separate but equal* is basically another term for segregation of the public schools, with, most commonly, black students going to one school and white students going to another. The schools were supposedly equal in quality, but, as this case brought to light, the schools were separate but rarely equal.

In *Brown v. the Board of Education*, the nation's Supreme Court reaffirmed the importance of education, and the role of government, in the following statement:

Today education is perhaps the most important function of the state and local governments. Compulsory school attendance laws and the great expenditures for education both demonstrate our recognition of the importance of education in a democratic society. It is required in the performance of our most basic public responsibilities . . . It is the very foundation of good citizenship. Today it is the principal instrument for awakening the child to cultural values, in preparing him for later professional training, and in helping him to adjust normally to his environment. In these days it is doubtful that any child may reasonably be expected to succeed if he is denied the opportunity of an education.

Public Education: A Local Responsibility

If the Supreme Court of the United States is correct, then one can readily understand the high interest in these questions: Who is responsible for the nation's schools? How should they be organized, administered and paid for? Let's take a closer look at how these issues have been addressed.

According to the *Statistical Abstract of the United States*, the projected enrollments of pupils in America's elementary and secondary schools for the year 1990 came to 29,373,000 in the elementary schools and 11,399,000 in the secondary schools. It was also projected that nearly $200 billion from federal, state and local funds would be spent on educating these children, with the state and local funding sources providing the bulk of the money. How is such a vast educational enterprise organized?

The founding fathers considered schooling to be of great importance to the nation, yet provision for the expense of education is not even mentioned in the Constitution of the United States. But this is not an oversight. Our Constitution established a federal government of limited powers: states hold onto those powers that affect the lives of their people most closely. States have authority in matters of local concern, and the federal government has authority in matters of national concern.

To be sure this would always be so, the Bill of Rights (in the Tenth Amendment) declares that: "The powers not delegated to the United States by the Constitution, nor prohibited by it to the States, are reserved to the States respectively or to the people." Since providing for the education of its people is not a power given to the federal government and is not one denied the states, education falls under the primary authority of the states—where it has remained to this day.

The states have always carefully guarded their authority over the schools. During the early days of the republic, when it was proposed that a national university be established, the motion was promptly defeated. As a result, the United States has no formally or legally protected national system of education. Instead, there are 50 state systems of education, each of which has authority over the schools within its borders.

It can be argued that education is the most important function of the states. Control of education in each state is delegated to local school districts. At one time there were as many as 30,000 school districts nationwide. In the interests of administrative efficiency, and to comply with the laws requiring racial balance in the schools, many districts have been consolidated over the years.

All states have an appointed or elected state superintendent of schools or some equivalent agency made up of citizens from various occupations. At the local or community level, each school district is governed by an elected or appointed school board, consisting of men and women from many fields who represent a wide range of experiences, concerns and viewpoints. Other state functions—police protection, highway building and regulation, determining health and hospital standards, to name a few—are mainly performed by professionally trained experts. School districts work in a different way. Authority for the schools is divided between a professional staff of administrators and teachers and a school board with members who are most likely not educators by profession. Because of this arrangement, local citizens have both the opportunity and the obligation to make the schools their children attend the best they can possibly be.

Within broad guidelines established by the states, local school districts have vast powers. They set tax rates, build new schools and refurbish old ones, set instructional policies and hire and fire school personnel. This is in keeping with the principles of the Constitution, in which the federal government has limited power over the daily lives of individuals. The common school was created to serve all students, yet no school district is precisely like any other. While all school districts have certain similarities in common with those within the state and even with those out of the state, each school district has a distinctive character of its own, reflecting the diverse backgrounds and goals of the people who live in it. Though local political issues can sometimes interfere with educational goals, community controlled schools can better understand, and respond to, their students.

Public Education as a Federal Responsibility

While the federal role in education is small compared with that of the states, federal interest in education has never been entirely absent. (It has grown dramatically since World War II to the present day.)

Government involvement in education has its roots in previous centuries. In establishing the government of the old Northwest, the present states of Ohio, Indiana, Illinois, Michigan, Wisconsin and part of Minnesota, Article 3 of the Northwest Ordinance of 1787 declared: "Religion, morality, and knowledge, being necessary for good government and the happiness of mankind, schools and the means of education shall forever be encouraged." Schools were encouraged by requiring that each township in the territories set aside a section of land (about one square mile) for the maintenance of public schools. Millions of acres of land were reserved in this way. The proceeds from the land's sale or the exploitation of mineral and agricultural resources from these properties provided important, and sometimes unexpected, sources of revenue.

In 1862, during the Civil War, Congress passed the Morrill Act. By its provisions, each state was granted 30,000 acres of public land for each of its members in Congress, the proceeds of which were to be used to establish a university devoted to the practical arts of agriculture and mechanics. The establishment of public universities brought higher education to new groups of students previously unable to afford expensive, privately funded colleges. They may be thought of as yet a further extension of the common school.

At the urging of President Andrew Johnson, the U.S. Office of Education was established in 1867, amid widespread opposition to federal interference in education. The purpose of the Office of Education, regulated by the Interior Department, was to collect data and to disseminate information about the management of schools to individual school districts. The first commissioner of education was Henry Barnard; he had urged such an organization for 30 years. The fear of allowing the federal government to interfere with community control of education has persisted, and creation of a department of education has long symbolized the fear of this control. It was not until 1979 that a separate, cabinet-level Department of Education was finally, but still reluctantly, established.

A federal presence in education has been perhaps most deeply felt in the last 20 years—with decisions of the U.S. Supreme Court on such issues as prayer in school, saluting the flag, providing for equalization of school financing and for school integration. Federal authority stems from the Preamble to the U.S. Constitution authorizing the government to "promote the general Welfare." Supreme Court decisions will be fully discussed in the next chapter. They became the laws of the land, with state and local governments responsible for administering their schools in compliance with them.

The Educational Ladder

The ladder system of education, referring to the progression of students from grade to grade, did not become widespread until the end of the 19th century. In 1872, a group of citizens in Kalamazoo, Michigan, sought to prevent its school board from collecting taxes for the purpose of establishing a high school. While the struggle for the common elementary school had, by and large, been won there, the citizens were by no means certain that authority existed for school boards to establish common, free high schools. A unanimous decision by the Michigan Supreme Court held that the board was acting properly and legally in imposing taxes for free secondary schools. Now looking back on that decision, it is clear that it paved the way for the common school to extend from the first through the 12th grade, with public funding.

Under the ladder system, a child would be promoted upon completion of the work of each grade. By standardizing the level of achievement necessary for gaining promotion, the ladder system was supposed to ensure that all students would be given an equal opportunity to learn and be evaluated. At least, this was the intent and the theory of those educational leaders who saw in the elementary and secondary schools an opportunity for all youth to improve their lives through schooling.

You are probably familiar with the educational ladder in your school district. However, the ladder in your district may be different from those in other school districts. Initially, the elementary school provided eight years of schooling and consisted of grades one through eight. The high school required four years of schooling and was made up of grades nine through 12. Based on ability, children were advanced from one grade to another. Those who did not appear to have the ability to move on were "left back," or "flunked," as we say now.

After experiments that began as early as 1870, many school districts began to offer parents the option of sending five-year-old children to kindergarten. This did not meet with the same level of resistance as compulsory high school. Early kindergartens were optional, and individual districts created them by choice rather than by state decree. Also, with the industrial revolution, more women were taking jobs in factories and offices, and kindergartens were a means of childcare. By 1918, kindergartens were widespread in many communities.

In response to the need to make the administration of schools more efficient and to respond to growing enrollments, the junior high school was developed. It was thought that in the junior high school—generally grades seven, eight and nine—children of the often difficult, early adolescent years could be helped to understand themselves, discover what society expects of them and work to best prepare themselves for further study, jobs or careers. Many educators believed that by targeting instruction at early adolescents, many more would be encouraged to go on to high school or at least be better prepared for their jobs. While the earlier model never disappeared entirely, by 1948 the most common ladder system was kindergarten through grade six for the elementary school, grades seven, eight and nine for the junior high school, and grades 10, 11 and 12 for the senior high school.

The junior high school proved to be a disappointment despite its widespread adoption. Children of this age group were regarded as especially difficult to teach, and the absence of both older and younger children as role models tended to exaggerate the emotional and physical growing pains of those years. Moreover, as larger numbers of children began to attend high schools automatically, the junior high school declined in popularity during the 1970s. A new intermediate school became a popular organizational form: The elementary school included kindergarten to grade four; the intermediate school, grades five through eight; and the high school, grades nine through 12.

Schools continue to be organized by grade levels, with the use of intermediate and junior high schools varying by school district. Some larger school districts, for example, have an intermediate school for grades six and seven, and a junior high school for grades eight and nine. Arrangements like this are often used to accommodate the sheer numbers of students at these grade levels, as opposed to specific educational reasons. It is difficult to determine whether or not tinkering with the educational ladder really improves the quality of education.

Early Philosophies of Education

As the common school movement spread, American educators continuously sought to learn more about how best to teach the nation's children. They examined not only school funding, community responsibility and the educational ladder but also how best to teach their students. In the work of a number of European philosophers, American educators found ideas they thought would be useful to the schools of the New World.

While schools in colonial America sought to educate by the rod, the Swiss philosopher Johann Heinrich Pestalozzi (1746–1827) taught that more could be accomplished with kindness and by understanding some of the ways in which a child's natural curiosity could be tapped in the instructional process. The German philosopher Friedrich Froebel (1782–1852) is often looked upon as the "father" of the kindergarten because in his view the best preparation for schooling was in the guided play of children. Johann Friedrich Herbart (1776–1841), a German psychologist as well as philosopher, insisted that the ultimate goal of education was the development of good character and moral behavior. He believed good character could best be taught by drawing on the interests of students while developing their intellect. To this day, his pattern for achieving these goals remains the basis of the "lesson plan" that many teachers are taught to develop for each lesson.

As the common school matured in the United States, many American philosophers of education also appeared to offer suggestions for the better schooling of children. Francis W. Parker (1837–1902), the principal of Cook County Normal School in Illinois, wrote *Talks on Pedagogics* (1899), in which he drew on what he believed to be the best of the European educational philosophers. His work helped Americans to shift the focus of education to the child rather than the subject. While a child must be taught reading, writing, history and other subjects, Parker suggested that to teach these subjects we must know a great deal about how the child learns and thinks. In that way, the child's imagination can best be captured. This is a sharp contrast from the colonial approach to education, with children in the early schools all memorizing the same information under the threat of verbal and physical punishment.

How much "child-centeredness" and how much "subject- centeredness"—or, more likely, how much of each to include—has been a perennial source of conflict in American education and never fully resolved. Should education be child-centered? Here, educators would focus on individual desires and needs, with each child allowed to proceed at his or her own pace. Or should education be subject-centered, focusing on the content of course offerings, with all students given the same set of specific expectations for their performance? These are important questions. And though our current educational system tends to be more subject-centered, this issue is by no means resolved to everyone's satisfaction as schools, teachers and administrators continuously strive to make the educational system even better.

American education has always functioned under stress. What is remarkable is that our system of education has constantly changed and improved and can rightfully claim responsibility for numerous achievements in our society.

Notes

Citations in the notes are brief. Full citations appear in the bibliography.

CHAPTER TWO

1. *Common School Journal*, Volume 1, 1839, 60.
2. Cremin, 1966.
3. Dewey.

CHAPTER THREE

The Achievements of the Nation's Schools

Americans have placed so much faith in their schools that education has been described as the nation's secular religion. In this chapter, we will take a closer look at this faith and what it means as we make judgments and decisions about schools. It is important to remember, however, that hard evidence—statistical relationships and trends—is not easy to find.

When American society is functioning at its best, economically and socially, the public schools are considered a success. When our society seems to be making major adjustments—during periods of social unrest or economic uncertainty, for example—the schools are often blamed, at least in part. Our faith in our schools becomes a mixed blessing when we look to them as a cure for any and all of America's problems.

Since schools are but one agency for the education of the public, it is very difficult to separate what the public schools alone achieve. Family and faith, library and museum, the work place and the leisure place, visual and print media, art and music, each of these plays a role in our education. The communities that we live in also play an important role. Because the schools are only one institution among many that teach, we look to the conclusion that Professor Lawrence Cremin draws:

"... the public school ought never to take the entire credit for the educational accomplishments of the public, and it ought never to be assigned the entire blame."[1]

Yet, as unfair as it seems, this is the situation that we as a society have created for our public schools.

The People and Their Schools

The effectiveness of today's schools is an easy target for widespread criticism. What may be surprising is that in survey after survey parents are satisfied with the schools their children attend. This paradox, which has been difficult to interpret, has also been demonstrated in research. In his book *A Place Called School*, John Goodlad reports on a survey of 8,624 parents— 1,724 whose children were in the elementary school, 2,688 whose children attended junior high schools and 4,212 whose children were at the senior high school level. Parents were asked to assign a grade to their schools of A, B, C, D or F (fail). Of those responding, only 10% gave their schools a D (7%) or an F (3%). By a wide majority, the parents responding gave the schools their children attend a good, solid B. Professor Goodlad reports, "Overall, the data do not convey the deep parental dissatisfaction that supposedly has prevailed widely." [2]

That parents do not give the schools a grade of A suggests they are aware that the schools their children attend are not perfect. However, while parents read about the shortcomings or problems in other schools, they apparently do not view their own children's schools as having any of these problems. This view is supported year after year in polls conducted annually by *Phi Delta Kappa*, a society of distinguished educators, and published annually in the society's journal, *Kappan*.

In a second study, Goodlad and his associates asked parents to rate the importance of the following four broad goals of education: (1) academic, embracing all intellectual skills and domains of knowledge; (2) vocational, geared to developing readiness for productive work and economic responsibility; (3) social and civic, related to preparing for socialization into a complex society; and (4) personal, emphasizing the development of individual responsibility, talent and free expression.[3]

Parents rated all four areas as "very important." Approximately 90% of the parents who responded gave academic goals this high rating. About 90% of the parents of elementary school children rated personal goals "very important," while 80% of those of junior and senior high school students assigned that rating. Vocational goals were rated only slightly lower by high school parents and somewhat lower by junior high parents. Social and civic goals were rated "very important" by 73% of the parents of elementary school children, with the percentage dropping to 66% and 64% at junior and senior high levels.[4] "The message here," Professor Goodlad concludes, "is that (parents) see as important all four of those goal areas which have emerged over the centuries and which had become well established in the rhetoric of educational expectations."[5]

The academic, the vocational, the civic and the personal goals of education were the mandates of the common school. These goals, however, must be reinterpreted in each generation. It is the triumph of American schooling that it has attempted to do so and has met with substantial success.

Let's take a closer look at how these goals developed in importance over the years.

Education for All

The common school's foremost goal was the education of the masses. This can be contrasted with the European view of education, which assumed that ability was a limited commodity, and that only those who were identified as having ability ought to be sent to school. In short, the European view was that it was not necessary to educate the masses. The French observer of the American commonwealth during the early 19th century, Alexis de Tocqueville, was astonished at how literate Americans were, and he questioned his own preference for the education of the elite to which he was accustomed in his country. He wrote, "A state of equality is perhaps less elevated, but it is more just: Its justice constitutes its greatness and its beauty." [6]

Horace Mann (1796–1859), who was America's leading educational pioneer, stressed that schools should be concerned with imparting knowledge to all students, rather than providing a liberal education for leaders: "The scientific or literary well-being of a community is to be estimated not so much by its possessing a few men of great knowledge, as its having many men of competent knowledge." [7] Even though the fight for free and universal public education was not quickly won, by the time of the American Civil War, these goals had gained wide acceptance among Americans. But universal education was still something of a novelty for European visitors to America, like de Tocqueville.

Although Horace Mann is the theorist of popular education, our realization of the practical benefits of Mann's theories can be credited to William Torrey Harris (1835–1909). A Connecticut-born educator, Harris put his administrative talents to work to make universal education possible, as superintendent of schools in St. Louis (1868–80) and as U.S. commissioner of education (1889–1906). Among his invaluable contributions were the organization of schools by grades; the collection of school statistics; the development of attendance reports; the selection and role of textbooks; the structure including the size, location, lighting and ventilation of school buildings; and the preparation of teachers.

Schooling and Literacy

Literacy and *numeracy* are terms that are not easily defined. For our purposes, however, they can be described as the basic ability to read and write, and the basic ability to use numbers, as in arithmetic. In a 1986 survey of the literacy of Americans 18 to 24 years old by the National Association of Educational Progress, nearly all (95%) were literate in that they could read, write and calculate.[8] Credit for achieving these high levels of basic, universal literacy must be given to the common schools.

When the American republic was young, a surprising number of Americans, especially those in towns and cities, could read and write at a competent level. This was evident during the months before the American Revolution, with arguments for and against separation from England appearing in newspapers and pamphlets, and posted in proclamations on the streets. Colonial Americans read this information and were incited to take action; the Revolution would not have been possible otherwise. As John Adams declared, "The American Revolution was effected before the war began. It was in the hearts and minds of the people." What he meant was that because so many could read, the idea had taken root. But illiteracy remained common in rural areas. For slaves and Indians, it was widespread. In colonial America, universal literacy had by no means been achieved.

Thomas Jefferson (1743–1826) recognized the need for every man to achieve literacy in his Rockfish Gap Report on the University of Virginia, of which he was founder (1819). This is his summary of the purposes of elementary education: (1) to give to every citizen the information he needs for the transaction of his own business; (2) to enable him to calculate for himself, and to express and preserve his ideas, his contracts and accounts, in writing; (3) to improve, by reading, his morals and faculties.[9] Education, according to Jefferson, was meant to help individuals achieve levels of literacy beyond what they could expect to acquire from family, community or religion. These ideas took hold with the birth of the common school. Universal literacy, it was believed, could reinforce democratic principles and augment the people's basic civil rights and liberties.

The common school contributed substantially to universal literacy, as was evident in the steadily rising literacy rate between 1870 and 1920. A *Fortune* magazine report on education (published in 1967) stated that while in 1899, "20 percent of the population over ten years of age was judged illiterate, this had fallen to just under eleven percent by 1900 and to 6 percent by 1920."[10] The rise in literacy continued, and by 1947, illiteracy had dropped to 2.7% for people aged 14 and over.[11]

In achieving basic literacy, *The New England Primer* (compiled by Benjamin Harris and first published before 1690), with more than 2 million copies printed, was the most widely used early reader in American schools before 1820. Noah Webster's (1758–1843) *Blue-Backed Speller* (1783) and later his *Grammar, Reader* and *Dictionaries* (during the early 1800s) helped children in the nation's early schools develop a national language. The famous William Holmes's (1800–73) *McGuffey Readers* also contributed to the widespread diffusion of reading skills in America.

In the course of great waves of European immigration in the 19th and 20th centuries, schools played a vital role in Americanizing the immigrant. It is true that labor unions and voluntary associations of many kinds contributed to this process. Nevertheless, it was the school's responsibility to teach English to newcomers and to instill in them the American way of life. Schools furnished immigrants with the skills that enabled them to participate effectively as citizens of the American republic and as workers in American industry. The larger purpose and outstanding achievement of American schools was to help its students to live in America. Schools contributed to the general literacy by providing children of immigrants with a civic language that allowed them to interact with the new world in which they lived.

By itself, basic universal literacy was certainly no guarantee of success in Jefferson's time, the early 1800s. But in colonial America, as is also true today, there lived a deeply held belief that without the skills to read and write, economic success remained unlikely either for the individual or for the nation. Colonial Americans held fast to the image of America as a place where education and hard work could yield unlimited possibilities. Of course, it did not hold true for all people. But the ideal was based on the uniquely American spirit and energy.

Early in our history, we developed the conviction that the stability, progress and financial success of America also depended on our ability to effectively pass on literacy skills to future generations, along with moral values such as work, thrift, industry, punctuality, perseverance and sacrifice. Because of this conviction, citizens were willing to tax themselves for the support of their public schools.

Today we are more realistic about the value of basic literacy. It is no longer enough for attaining success; our society has become too fast paced and complex even to get by, not to mention excel, with only the ability to read basic books and perform simple arithmetic. Yet, many in our society lack even these rudimentary skills. How to best help those who are functionally illiterate is a growing problem and an important issue for the public schools.

Schooling and the American Economy

Horace Mann (1796–1859) viewed support from the business community as an important ingredient for the growth of the common school. In seeking to enlist this support, he assured businesspeople that schools would encourage respect for private property, expand wealth, provide industry with efficient workers and preserve order. The contribution of our public schools to the general economy is complex and difficult to quantify. It is nearly impossible to attach numerical values to measure the cause and effects of education. However, even in the absence of complex economic formulas, there is general agreement that no first-rate economy is possible without first-rate schools.

From the beginning, Americans regarded schools as the chief means of achieving equality of opportunity and enhancing upward social mobility. As a result of this belief, classroom subjects became paired with teachings about moral virtues such as thrift, punctuality and perseverance. These make up the so-called Horatio Alger view of upward mobility. Horatio Alger (1832–99) was a Unitarian minister who wrote numerous novels about young boys who rose from rags to riches through their effort and persistence.

The common school, because it taught children the skills and virtues necessary for success in business, has been credited with making upward mobility attainable for poor Americans. This theme has been seriously questioned in recent years, particularly in light of racial and ethnic prejudice, the lingering effects of poverty and changes in the job market resulting from periodic recessions. Yet, the consensus of opinion today is that for nearly all groups the school has played some part in making upward mobility possible.

Our educational system really reflects the values of our society as a whole, and as students learn these values they also learn what it takes to move forward and excel in society as adults. Admittedly, this reflection of mainstream American values has helped some groups more than others. Schools were far more accessible to whites than blacks and Native Americans, for example. The American-born initially benefited more than the immigrant. Those who were born into more comfortable circumstances enjoyed more of the benefits of schooling than did those who were born into impoverished families. Clearly, schools did not make all students equally prosperous men and women. But it cannot be denied that the public school played a significant role in improving living standards for most of those who attended.

During the second half of the 19th century, the school's role began to expand beyond literacy, to encompass vocational education as well. America needed skilled workers for its growing factories, and the schools provided the skilled workers needed to keep industry moving. However, the importance of vocational education was not clear until Americans realized what other countries were doing to prepare their students for the workplace. In 1876, the United States held a great Centennial Exposition in Philadelphia that included exhibits from other countries. The exhibits clearly demonstrated America was a formidable force in industrial technology. Credit for America's growing preeminence was given to the ideal relationship between education and the national economy. During the Centennial Exhibition, the Russians stood out among other European countries, with exhibits that demonstrated various techniques for teaching carpentry and other "manual arts." Russia was undergoing its own industrial development, and the schools were playing an integral role in preparing students with needed work skills. As a result, widespread interest developed in how to incorporate technical education into the growing common school movement.

Calvin M. Woodward (1860–1930) emerged as the foremost advocate for manual arts training in American common schools. He conceived an approach whereby manual training was to be incorporated into the academic preparation of all children in order to acquaint them with the work world. The manual arts consisted of courses such as "shop" and home economics, in which students were given an opportunity to try their hands at work- and home-related tasks for a short time each day. This approach was initially thought of as a means of improving the manual skills of students and broadening their overall development, rather than as vocational or skilled training for a particular job. As industry moved beyond the use of simple tools to more complex machinery, however, the manual arts became vocational training, as a means of providing industry with competent mechanics.

By 1910, vocational education had won support from such groups as the National Association of Manufacturers as well as from the initially skeptical American Federation of Labor. The National Education Association and various farm associations agreed on the importance of vocational education to the continued growth of American superiority in industry and agriculture.

Expenditures on schools may be called society's investment in human capital. Economists, such as Theodore W. Schultz (b. 1902), have concluded that this investment is as important to the nation's economic growth as investment in nonhuman capital such as machinery, railroads and nuclear power plants. Schultz concluded that during the formative years of American education, between 1929 and 1957, real national income in the United States ("real" means that the numbers have been adjusted for inflation and the rise in prices that occurs over time) rose from $150 billion to $302 billion. Schultz concluded that, "As a source of economic growth, the additional schooling of the labor force would appear to account for about one-fifth of the rise in real national income in the United States. . ."[12]

American Education and Patriotism

Patriotism can be defined as the love people have for their country, either the country they were born in or the one to which they have chosen to give allegiance. Patriotism encompasses love of land and love of familiar customs and unique traditions. For Americans, the terms *patriotism, nationalism* and *loyalty* are all interrelated.

With the successful end of the American Revolution, it was clear in the minds of the nation's founders that a distinctively American educational system needed to be developed. The family, the church, the press, voluntary associations and business institutions, along with the schools, were all to play a role in the educational network that would make a unique American civilization possible. School children needed to learn about the history of their own nation and people to develop an allegiance to their country.

The American flag gradually became a symbol of the school's role in encouraging patriotism. During the War of 1812, the flag was flown for the first time over an American schoolhouse. It was during the Civil War that the practice of flying the American flag on the roofs of schoolhouses actually became widespread. This symbolic joining of the American flag with American schools demonstrates the close tie that education has forged with the growth and development of patriotism in the United States.

The outward symbol of the flag also demonstrated what was going on inside the school. As common schools grew in number and in importance, America added yet another responsibility to the long list for common schools: Not only would boys and girls learn about their country and embrace patriotism, schools were now expected to motivate students to a willingness to defend their nation against any who would attack or undermine it. American history became an obvious vehicle for encouraging this level of patriotism.

The U.S. Constitution, in effect, created a country—founded by a group of renegades—out of a vast wilderness. It was critical that all citizens understand the principles and values of the Constitution, if these concepts were to be perpetuated. The common school was the natural place to assure that Constitutional values were taught.

The current leadership role that teachers have in developing patriotism in their students has its roots in earlier days of the common school. Teachers were given the duty to become well acquainted with America's history—and not only to pass on what they learned to their students but to do it in a way that would inspire a sense of national unity and patriotism. In 1837, the College of Teachers in Cincinnati voted in favor of making American history a required subject of study in the common schools. The college also urged that schools help students to develop an understanding of the United States Constitution, along with an awareness of how the government works, the nature of its laws and the need for obedience to those laws.

American history textbooks told of the heroic work of the Founding Fathers and spoke of the unique mission of America in bringing liberty and justice to all humankind. These textbooks include passages extolling America as the land of opportunity, the cradle of liberty, the birthplace of democracy, the land of the free and the home of the brave. Civic virtue was praised, as was the heroism of American soldiers. Assembly programs, school plays, inspirational prose, poetry and music served to reinforce patriotic zeal.

The school's function in encouraging patriotism went beyond the history and civics classes. The school also identified those aspects of language, literature, music, art, government and in some cases, science as well as arithmetic, which were or could be portrayed as distinctively American. Readers, grammars, geographies and spellers all contained references to the merits of the American form of government—portraying it as better and more caring than any other. Noah Webster's work is a good example. In his dictionary and spellers, popularized after the Revolution, Webster's goal was to develop a distinctly American language that would systematize and organize the customary American vocabulary, spelling and grammar. By winning acceptance for a common, standard usage of American English, he hoped to help unify the nation. With a unified American language that differentiated American English from the English that had been imposed on the colonies by England, it was assumed that national unity and devotion would follow.

At the same time that an American English came into its own, the United States was also growing into its own national identity. By the time major waves of immigrants from countries throughout Europe (all with their own languages and customs) arrived at these shores in the mid to late 19th century, the American culture and school system were ready to play a key role in their integration into life in the United States.

Education was not limited to the mastery of the English language. Schools taught the nature of American democracy and practiced it as well. Perhaps more than other institutions, they came close to embodying the ideals of American democracy. In the environment of the school, opportunity was to be provided for all, based on merit and accomplishments—regardless of race, class, wealth or power.

Our current public school system is evidence of how schools have continued to thrive as microcosms of democracy. During the 20th century, the school and classroom came to be organized to give students some experience in choosing class and school officers, voting in elections for these posts, editing a school newspaper, and in some cases, handling money used by clubs and athletic teams. Through such class- and school-wide extracurricular activities, students are encouraged to form the habits expected of responsible citizens. These habits include voting in elections, becoming candidates for public office, listening to more than one point of view, valuing free speech and press, accepting the decision of majority rule as determined by the outcome of a secret ballot and respecting minority rights. Thus, the schools have encouraged habits of civic virtue and reinforced democratic principles.

Even in an educational system as diverse as ours, with each local school district making many of its own decisions, the public schools have helped to develop loyalty to the nation as a whole. One might think these diverse and locally supported schools would generate divided loyalties to particular towns, villages, cities or states. While these separate loyalties are present—as is evident at every Saturday afternoon high school football game—the larger patriotism encouraged by the schools of each state is to the nation as a whole.

Schools continue to provide the function of "Americanizing" the new immigrants. Yet at the same time, the very notion of Americanization recognizes diversity among people. It is now the schools' responsibility to instill pride among children in the land and the language of their parents and ancestors, while at the same time helping them to adapt to the American culture. This is the essence of patriotism. And as we approach the 21st century, our nation is experiencing new waves of immigrants from Spanish-speaking countries, as well as from Korea and other Asian countries. Through example, persuasion, instruction and participation, public school classrooms will continue to introduce newcomers to the American way of life, while also recognizing and learning from their students' heritage.

Schooling improved literacy, spurred the American economy and helped unify a diverse nation, but schooling benefits more than the learner. Each driver is safer if all the others can read traffic signs. Everyone benefits from a more responsive government if all voters have the capacity to use their vote intelligently. Each person in a community will be healthier if everyone knows about and observes the basic rules of sanitation. From this we can conclude that education is a powerful engine of economic growth, social mobility and national cohesion.

During the second half of the 20th century, we as Americans have seriously questioned and debated the concept of equal opportunity, both past and present. The school system, from both a historical and current perspective, has certainly not escaped examination.

In response to the question: "Who should be taught?", the founders of the common school replied, "All children." Yet, as we look back on the early days of education, did "all" mean women as well as men? Blacks and Indians as well as whites? The poor as well as the better off? The sick? The mentally and physically impaired? How the nation responded to these questions and what remains to be done is the subject of the next chapter.

Notes

Citations in the notes are brief. Full citations appear in the bibliography.

CHAPTER THREE

1. Cremin, 1976, 58.
2. Goodlad, 36.
3. Ibid., 37.
4. Ibid.
5. Ibid., 38.
6. Tocqueville, 350–51.
7. Mann, 315.
8. Kirsch and Jungeblut.
9. Honeywell, 248–60.
10. Butts and Cremin, 408.
11. Ibid., 569.
12. Schultz, 11.

CHAPTER FOUR

Who Should Be Taught?

$\mathbf{F}$rom its earliest history, the American educational system has reflected the values of the society at large. As you saw in Chapter Three, American values of each era determined how vocational skills, religion and patriotism were presented in the classroom. For better or worse, these values have also determined who was taught. On the one hand, the American belief in education for the masses led to compulsory education, which ensured that a wide spectrum of children and young adults of school age could attend school and not enter the work force full-time. On the other hand, the country's way of life at the time made segregation a fact. But as American values changed, so did the schools. Ultimately, more enlightened thinking resulted in racially integrated schools, bilingual education and better facilities for the handicapped.

Compulsory Education

Urged by educators and, slowly but surely, encouraged by state legislators, each state in the union adopted a plan of compulsory education. Massachusetts was the first state (1852), and Mississippi the last (1918), to require that all children be sent to school. One of the stumbling blocks to enacting compulsory education was the question of whether states could force parents to send their children to public school. In the Oregon case of *Pierce v. The Society of Sisters of Jesus and Mary* (1925), the United States Supreme Court held that Oregon could not require parents to send their children to public schools. They could, if they wished, send their children to independent or parochial schools. Public education is supported by tax dollars. Independent schools are secular and are supported mostly by tuition payments from the parents whose children attend. Parochial schools are related to a religious institution (i.e., church, synagogue, mosque) and are usually also supported by tuition from parents.

The years of compulsory school attendance varied widely. Some states required children to stay in school until age 14 while others insisted upon instruction until age 18. The differences in ages depended upon local conditions, the importance the state attached to public schooling and the willingness of states to tax themselves for funding higher grades.

Passing compulsory education laws was one thing; enforcing them was another. For many years, enforcement was lax, especially where children could be made to work at low wages in factories or on farms. Following World War I, however, compulsory attendance laws were more strictly enforced. Educators and legislators became aware of how important additional years of schooling were to the nation's economy and democratic traditions. Laws protecting children from working excessive hours under dangerous conditions meant young people could remain in school and prepare themselves for better opportunities in the future.

High school enrollments doubled in the 1920s and doubled again in the 1930s. By 1940, there was ample evidence that progress was being made toward the central goal of the common school: educating all the children of all the people. The average American adult had at that time completed 8.6 years of schooling. Those between the ages of 25 and 29 had completed 10.3 years. The expectation became widespread that nearly all children would complete elementary school and go on to some secondary school. About half the 17- and 18-year-olds actually did complete high school.

Enrollments in grades nine to 12, as a representative percentage of Americans aged from 14 to 17, rose from 73% in 1940 to 93% in 1971 and has fluctuated between 90% and 94% since then. In 1968–69, the number of high school graduates, as a percentage of all 17-year-olds, reached a high of 77%, fell to 71% in 1979–80 and rose again to 74% in 1988–89. Add the number of people who earned diplomas through programs of adult education, and the overall percentage of high school graduates would be 85% to 86% of the population.[1]

At first glance, these figures certainly look gratifying. The dreams of Horace Mann and his colleagues and latter-day disciples appear to have been realized. In truth, however, these data did not tell the whole story. As noted earlier, the fact is that Horace Mann had little to say about the education of women and nothing at all to say about the schooling of blacks, Native Americans and other ethnic or racial minorities. The blinders worn by the founders of the common school were to become fatal flaws in the fabric of American schooling, undermining the myth that the public schools were, in reality, offering equal educational opportunity to the children of all American parents.

Many more men completed high school than women; those from affluent families did so far more frequently than those from poor ones; whites were more likely to complete high school than other racial groups. Northern children were more likely to finish than southern, while urban adolescent graduates exceeded rural ones. As Colin Greer, a historian of education who questions whether schools have *ever* really been open to all, noted in 1972, "The public schools have never really embraced the mass of the community, nor do they now."[2]

The Poor Fall Through the School Network

While Horace Mann assured the power brokers of his day that free, common schools would be "the great equalizer" of the people's condition, American schools did not fully achieve the goals of being common or equal. Many American communities were essentially homogeneous—that is, made up of families similar in race and ethnicity (national origins) and without extremes of wealth and poverty. The schools served these communities well. In fact, the perceived success of the common school nationwide was based largely on what the schools appeared to be accomplishing in these homogeneous communities: making children proficient in the three Rs, preparing them to work effectively in local business and industry and instilling a patriotic devotion to the state and nation.

But where the community was made up of urban or rural poor, or contained a substantial number of recently arrived immigrant groups, the common school failed to measure up to the expectations of its proponents. While myth has it that schools were the major factor in the acculturation of the rural poor and European immigrant to urban areas, in reality poverty often kept these students from taking full advantage of the school system. Impoverished immigrant families often depended upon the wages of all family members, including the children. It was frequently impossible for these students to fit themselves to the mold of monolithic (inflexible) schools and their rigid routines. To many, the school was an obstacle course to get past, instead of a ladder to economic success.

For many immigrant groups, school was initially an institution that threatened their religious and secular traditions and appeared to strike at the roots of family and social structure. Teachers and principals did not always understand the traditions that the immigrants and rural poor brought with them to the schools and sometimes even labeled these traditions "un-

American." This ignorance further alienated the newcomer who sought an education in the common school. Thus, children who, for example, were black, impoverished or recent immigrants were forced to fit a pre-existing mold of behavior and learning. Those who failed to do so were left to fend for themselves with schools making little effort to adjust or adapt their programs and activities to serve the needs of *all* their students.[3]

Leonard Covello, an Italian immigrant who later became a prominent principal of a New York City high school, colorfully summarized the plight of the immigrant: "We were becoming Americans by learning how to be ashamed of our parents."[4] If the price of going to school in America meant that children would be encouraged to mock or abandon the ways and traditions of their parents, then the price to many immigrants seemed excessive. As a result, it was not until the second or even third generation that immigrant poor began to take advantage of free, common schools to improve their living standard.

This struggle to serve *all* students honorably is not yet resolved. But in recent years, as Americans, we have developed a greater understanding of our varied backgrounds and can now champion the diversity of our culture. More importantly, we are seeking ways of identifying and accommodating diversity in our classrooms.

If schools seem to achieve remarkable results for some, even a substantial number of children, why can't they do so for all children—including those from the urban and rural poor and racial minorities? State and national authorities continue to hammer out an effective program to embrace an ever larger number of children, many of whom, through no fault of their own, appear more difficult to teach than those who come from "mainstream" America. Equality of educational opportunity means that all schools are funded at similar levels and all children have equal access to the best education that money can buy. But the dilemma of public education is this: Since it is based on local control and because some communities are willing and able to tax themselves more heavily than others in support of their schools, some districts are better supported than others.

Moreover, even if schools are funded equally, the quality of the education received may be unequal. That is, some children simply learn more than others. Some children are smarter, some more diligent, some more motivated. To what extent, if any, are schools responsible for equality of results as well as for equality of funding and access?

Defining the responsibilities of the public schools, as we have seen, is complicated. Also complicated is the process of measuring and evaluating how those responsibilities are carried out. The issue of equality of results comes to the surface periodically, often in relation to initiatives to require high school seniors to pass comprehensive tests before they are allowed to graduate. These initiatives are occasionally introduced by state legislators but are generally opposed by both educators and minority groups who question the fairness and validity of the tests. Equality of results is also discussed in relation to the testing of teachers and to questions over federal and state funding for poorer school districts.

There is little disagreement, however, that students should have the opportunity to learn on an even instructional field, regardless of race, economics or other factors, with the schools providing equal opportunity for each student to excel as far as his or her intellectual powers permit.

Separate but Unequal

The post–Civil War amendments to the Constitution freed the slaves (Amendment Thirteen), made the former slaves citizens (Amendment Fourteen), and gave them the right to vote (Amendment Fifteen). The Fourteenth Amendment, adopted in

1868, also provided that, "No State shall make or enforce any law which shall abridge the privileges or immunities of citizens of the United States; nor shall any State deprive any person within its jurisdiction the equal protection of the laws." It is the latter, the "equal protection" clause, that has been the constitutional basis for providing equal educational opportunity for black Americans.

Because educating slaves had been illegal in the Confederacy, the end of the Civil War meant Northern educators could devote themselves in earnest to the schooling of former slaves. As early as 1862, when President Abraham Lincoln issued the Emancipation Proclamation, freeing slaves in the states that had left the Union, the New England Freedmen's Aid Society sent 72 teachers to Port Royal, Virginia, to begin the task of teaching blacks. The abolitionist American Missionary Society followed up each Union victory by sending teachers into the South. By the war's end, some 353 teachers were hard at work teaching reading, writing and arithmetic to former slaves. Other organizations were no less vigorous in their educational mission to the newly emancipated people. The Bureau of Refugees, Freedmen, and Abandoned Lands, established in 1865, was responsible for providing for the health, welfare and education of former slaves during the period of Southern Reconstruction (1865–76). Of the myriad aspects of the mission of the Freedmen's Bureau, as it was generally called, nothing was more important to its leadership than providing for the schooling of the recently emancipated people.

The defeated Confederates felt the Northern "do-gooders" were intruders who did not understand the mind, culture or temperament of the South. The Northern schoolmarm (teachers were mostly women) was perceived to be judgmental of Southerners, conducting herself with a great deal of insensitivity to Southern pride. This was not helpful in soliciting the essential cooperation of proud Southern men and women who had just lost a war. When these teaching missionaries from the North sought to educate black and white children in the same school, for instance, Southerners became outraged, especially since most Northern schools were segregated by race.

When Southerners heard Northern schoolteachers encouraging former slaves to sing "Marching Through Georgia," a song memorializing Union General William Tecumseh Sherman's destructive march from Atlanta, Georgia, to the sea, they felt that their open wounds were being rubbed with salt. Little wonder, then, that teaching missionaries often found themselves in a hostile and sometimes dangerous environment.

Attitudes were slow to soften. If the defeated Confederacy had its way former slaves would not be equal to white people. To protect themselves from the good intentions of Northern teachers and to keep the freed slaves in subordinate roles, every state in the former Confederate Union, except Tennessee, passed Black Codes forcing black Americans to perform only the most menial of tasks for inadequate wages. Blacks could not travel, nor could they vote in state elections, carry arms or serve on juries. The Black Codes, which were repealed by the end of Reconstruction in 1876, had the effect of imposing a new kind of slavery. In a paradoxical way, since "masters" were no longer held directly responsible for the welfare of slaves they owned, the freed men and women were especially vulnerable to random attacks by bands of white hoodlums as well as by white supremacist organizations, such as the Ku Klux Klan and the Knights of the White Camellia. So much violence against freed blacks erupted that the distinguished historian John Hope Franklin (b. 1915) described the period as "an open season on Negroes."

In 1876, Reconstruction ended and federal troops were withdrawn from the South. Still, the former Confederacy was unwilling to relinquish the racial patterns of the Old South. Despite the Fifteenth Amendment, Southern states wrote new constitutions disenfranchising (denying the vote to) the blacks. The new state constitutions included "Jim Crow" laws, which separated blacks and whites so each race had to use separate cars on trains, waiting rooms, water fountains and rest rooms, parks and eating facilities, hotels, barbershops, theaters, restaurants and, of course, schools. Blacks were segregated publicly and privately from whites as "Jim Crow" became the accepted practice.

In 1875, Congress had passed the Civil Rights Act, which guaranteed all citizens full and equal privileges at inns, restaurants, transportation facilities, theaters and schools. Nor were blacks to be excluded from serving on juries. However, in 1883, the U.S. Supreme Court declared, in the Civil Rights Cases (109 U.S.3), that the Civil Rights Act of 1875 was unconstitutional. Denial of such privileges, the Court held, was not discrimination. While the Fourteenth Amendment prohibited states from discriminating on the basis of race, individuals and private corporations were not so prohibited. The Fifth, Thirteenth and Fourteenth Amendments, the courts insisted, protected the individuals in their political rights but not in their "social" rights.

In 1896, the Supreme Court carried Jim Crow policies even further when in *Plessy v. Ferguson* the Court upheld a Louisiana law requiring separate facilities for whites and blacks in railroads. Although the accommodations were separate, the Court held that if they were "equal," then this segregation was permissible. The Supreme Court majority held that, "If enforced separation of the two races stamps the colored race with a badge of inferiority, it is not anything found in the act, but solely because the colored race chooses to put that construction upon it."

The evidence that separate but equal was untrue is most obvious in the schools. Schools for blacks were inferior in physical condition, training and salaries of teachers, age and condition of textbooks and in availability of instructional equipment. Above all, expenditures per pupil were far lower in schools for blacks than for whites.

In attempting to make the best of a bad situation, Booker T. Washington (1856–1915), the founder of Tuskegee Institute, tried to work within the framework of a segregated society. He urged blacks to acquire useful and practical skills so when they "proved" themselves, they would be accepted by whites as equals. The two races were like different fingers of the same hand, he said, separate but indispensable to one another. This approach, shared by many other educators, had the ultimate effect of keeping blacks in a subordinate role. Washington was accused of failing to resist segregation and racial discrimination more aggressively. W. E. B. Du Bois (1868–1963), on the other hand, founded the National Association for the Advancement of Colored People (NAACP) in 1909. This organization was established precisely for the purpose of vigorously fighting segregation and bringing it to an end.

In 1945, the U.S. Senate Committee on Education and Labor began hearings on a controversial proposal to provide federal aid to education. The proposal was controversial because the need for the federal government to take any role in public education was not yet understood or accepted. Now federal aid to education, while not large, is no longer controversial. In 1945, those who opposed the aid feared that along with federal funds would come federal control of the schools and the slow erosion of local and state authority over educational policy. Moreover, those hostile to federal aid to education did not like the idea that additional funds would be provided to schools educating black children.

Those who favored authorizing federal assistance, including the National Education Association and the NAACP, felt that it would help repair the gross inequality between rural and urban schools and especially between the education available to blacks and whites. During Senate hearings, a number of teachers were called upon to provide firsthand descriptions of what it was really like in the classrooms where they taught. What follows are two poignant excerpts from their testimony, illustrating—much better than any statistics could—the glaring inequalities among schools that existed at that time.

Miss Wilma Upchurch, a white teacher from rural Nebraska, reported that her school of 487 pupils had 12 teachers; only seven held college degrees. Salaries were low, teacher turnover was high, as much as 50%, and one out of every five teachers in the state had emergency certificates because they lacked proper qualifications. Her poor school district taxed itself to the limit, yet could spend only $40 to $47 annually per pupil. "I am sure I could get a job in another state, or maybe I could work at the bomber plant," Miss Upchurch testified, "but I would rather stay in the teaching profession. Somebody has got to teach those children, and I would like to do it."

Mrs. Florence Christmas, a black teacher from Copiah County, Mississippi, described her school of 190 children and three teachers. As principal, she taught all subjects in grades five through eight and received $360 for six months. The other two teachers received $292 and $288 for six-month terms. Of 6,000 black teachers in Mississippi, 5,000 received less than $600 per school year. In Copiah County, the average salary for white teachers was $889.53 per term while that for black teachers was $332.58. White school children attended school for eight months, black children only six. Of the 91 white teachers in the county, 44 had no college degrees. For the 126 black teachers, 122 had no college degrees. When Mrs. Christmas was not teaching, she worked in a factory making containers for vegetables where she earned almost as much in a week as in a month of teaching. Senator William Fulbright of Arkansas asked, "Why do you do teaching?" She replied, "Teaching is my profession. I would rather teach."[5]

A Turning Point

As World War II came to a close, the contributions of black soldiers were evident. They played a key role in the war, as well as in earlier wars. And equally apparent was the discrimination that continued throughout the nation.

One million blacks had served in the armed forces. They defended democracy but were themselves discriminated against by their government even as they risked their lives. When stationed in the South, blacks were humbled by legally authorized segregation. When they went North, they saw that in at least some communities, the races need not live altogether apart. When they fought overseas, they discovered that in some countries, American-style racism was unknown.

In 1944, the Swedish sociologist Gunnar Myrdal (1898–1987) published *An American Dilemma*, which contained a scathing indictment of America's treatment of blacks. According to Myrdal, the "American dilemma" was that racial prejudice and discrimination could not be reconciled with the ideals of freedom, opportunity, justice, equality and liberty. Ultimately, he said, "the survival in modern American society of the slavery institution," had to be eliminated.[6]

Leading educators recognized that fairness required that racial factors should play no part with regard to school admission. How could it be otherwise?

Making Schools Color Blind

It was a crucial moment in American history when a car pulled to the curb and the door opened for two black children. They stepped onto the sidewalk and with tense, fearful faces began the long, frightening walk to the entrance of Central High School in Little Rock, Arkansas. On either side of them a seemingly endless gauntlet of jeering whites was held at bay by soldiers.

For the first time in this school's existence, a black child crossed the threshold in search of an elusive prize: the right to an education equal to that of whites. This prize was made possible by the decision of the United States Supreme Court in 1954. In the case of *Brown v. the Board of Education of Topeka, Kansas,* it declared segregated schools inherently inferior and laws segregating schools by race unconstitutional.

Before the 1954 *Brown* ruling, both northern and southern schools were segregated by race. There was, however, an important difference between segregated schools in the South and in the North. In the South, schools were segregated by law (*de jure*). That is, Jim Crow legislation required schools in the South to be segregated and made it illegal for whites and blacks to be taught in the same school facility. In the North, no legislation demanded that segregated schools be established; blacks and whites were separated under the concept of neighborhood schools. If children were to be sent to the schools nearest their parents' home, then those children residing in all-white neighborhoods generally went to all- or nearly all- white schools. This is described as *de facto* segregation. *De facto* in this situation meant that although there were no laws to mandate segregation, the effect was still the same as if there had been.

Former Democratic Senator from Connecticut Abraham Ribicoff declared in 1970, "Massive school segregation does not exist because we have segregated our schools, but because we have segregated our society and our neighborhoods. That is the source of the inequality, the tension and the hatred that disfigure our nation. . . ."[7]

The Brown Case and Its Aftermath

The Court's decision in the *Brown* case was a further refinement of the common school. It cleared the way for more effective schooling. Still, removing the tattered remnants of prejudice would require years of agitation and physical and legal battles.

A year later, for example, in 1955, the Court returned to the *Brown* decision and left the implementation to local authorities and local courts. School authorities and courts were directed "to admit to public schools on a racially nondiscriminatory basis with all deliberate speed the parties to these cases." By leaving implementation to local agencies, the Court assured that each community would determine for itself the "deliberate speed" with which it would act to end racially segregated schools. Some districts dragged their feet.

By 1964, fewer than 2% of black students in the 11 states of the South went to school with whites. However, that year Congress passed and President Lyndon Johnson signed the Civil Rights Act, the Economic Opportunity Act, followed by the Elementary and Secondary Education Act in 1965. This legislation collectively marked a new and more vigorous role for the federal government in the battle against race consciousness in America.

Title Six of the Civil Rights Act forbade discrimination in any federally funded program. Federal funds were to be cut from any program found to exhibit illegal discrimination. As many southern senators feared, this provision enabled the federal government to deny funds to schools otherwise slated to be funded under the Elementary and Secondary Education Act, a federal funding program for schools. A year after Title Six was enforced, significant progress was made in achieving racial integration in schools in the South. Integration in schools rose from 2% to 6% and 1,563 school districts embarked upon school desegregation programs. In a single year, more school districts began the move to desegregation than in the entire decade between 1954 and 1964.

But the federal government was still dissatisfied. In 1966, it established new criteria that had to be met before a school district could be considered integrated and thereby entitled to federal funds. As federal activism grew, so did resistance in Congress among northern as well as southern senators and representatives.

Congressional backlash was met by a more activist court as federal judges worked to define what, in practical terms, the *Brown* decision really required. A breakthrough was achieved in the Fifth Circuit Court of Appeals in the case of *Singleton v. Jackson Municipal Separate School District* (1970). Judge John Minor Wisdom upheld the Department of Health, Education and Welfare guidelines: It was not enough for school districts to demonstrate they were not discriminating on the basis of race, they had to show they were actually integrating schools. To dodge the full impact of the *Brown* decision, many school districts contended that if schools were all black or all white, it was essentially because blacks and whites "chose" to attend these schools and the resulting pattern of racial distribution had nothing to do with racial discrimination. "Not good enough," the courts in effect held. The U.S. Constitution required public schools, as Judge Wisdom wrote, "to integrate students, facilities, and activities."

Judge Wisdom supported the use of racial percentages to achieve integration. "The only school desegregation plan that meets Constitutional standards is one that works," insisted Wisdom. Judge Wisdom's decision affected both southern and northern schools, prodding school districts into speeding the integration process. "By 1968, the proportion had grown to 32 percent, and by 1972, 91 percent of Southern black students attended school with whites."[8]

The Coleman Report

In the urban cities of the North, *de facto* segregated schools appeared unaffected. But was this fair? Was it right and moral for schools in the South to be desegregated and those in the North to retain their racial composition? Since segregation in northern schools appeared to be based on housing patterns and not on laws, it seemed as if they could not be forced to integrate. In 1966, the U.S. Office of Education issued a ponderous report called *Equality of Educational Opportunity*, commonly referred to as the Coleman report after the man who headed the research team. The report was prepared in compliance with the Civil Rights Act of 1964, which required an investigation of the "lack of equal educational opportunities" for individuals by reason of race, color, religion or national origin in American public institutions. Led by James S. Coleman of Johns Hopkins University, the team investigated differences in school achievement among 575,000 pupils in 4,000 schools across the country.

So surprising and disappointing were the results of this pivotal study that the U.S. Office of Education released the report on July Fourth weekend so it would draw little scrutiny from a public intent on summer vacations and Independence Day festivities. Yet the report, 737 pages long with a 548-page statistical appendix, shocked the educational community if not the nation. The essentials of the report can be summarized as follows:

1. Most American pupils attended schools where almost all other students were of the same race.
2. "American schools were virtually separate and equal" at the time of the survey. That is, while white students attended schools somewhat better in physical condition than those attended by blacks, the *physical* differences were far fewer than anticipated.
3. By grade one, minority children were one to two years behind whites in terms of skills and knowledge they were expected to have mastered. By grade 12, minority children were as much as three to five years behind whites in educational achievement.

4. Most shocking was the assertion that the difference in educational attainment had nothing to do with per-pupil expenditures, pupil-teacher ratios, age and quality of physical facilities or books in the library. How much students learned was related to family background rather than to school quality.

5. After family background, the social composition of the school and the students' sense of control in their environment served to explain success. These factors were considered more important than school facilities, books and teachers in explaining differences in pupil achievement.

The grave implications of the Coleman report are still being debated. Books and monographs as long as the report were churned out in an attempt to diffuse its impact and the implication, an erroneous one, that schools themselves did not make a difference in how much students learn. While we will come back to other implications of the Coleman report in another chapter, from the point of view of school integration, the report was significant. Even though the Coleman report denied that spending more on school facilities would help improve student achievement, it did acknowledge that integration might substantially improve the performance of minority children. The report indicated that, "in the long run, integration should be expected to have a positive effect on Negro achievement."

The report seemed to imply that racial integration would improve black performance. But on a more controversial level, the report also seemed to imply that a white majority was necessary to make integration successful. While these points continue to be the subject of much controversy, when the report was first issued it appeared to provide ammunition enough for those who believed that northern, urban schools could not remain segregated by race.

Many northern school districts followed the lead of the New York City Board of Education, which held that "racially homogeneous schools damage the personality of minority group children," "decrease their motivation" and "impair their ability to learn." The board pledged to end *de facto* segregation in the city schools. In order to achieve desegregated schools, children were bused from their homes to schools sometimes a fair distance from where they lived. Busing of children became, in itself, a controversial issue for black as well as white parents. The concept of neighborhood schools seemed to clash with the goal of integrated schools.

In 1967, responding to a request of President Johnson, the U.S. Commission on Civil Rights issued a report titled *Racial Isolation in the Public Schools*. The report confirmed and went beyond the Coleman report in insisting upon an end to racial isolation in the public schools of America. It offered two remedies to help black children succeed in school: (1) provide additional instruction, often called compensatory education, or (2) disperse black and other minority children in white majority schools. The preferred remedy for poor performance of minority children was the latter. The report appeared to suggest that, not only was dispersion preferable as an approach to improve black and minority achievement, but it was also considered less expensive than funds for compensatory and other special forms of instruction. The report underestimated the potential difficulties of achieving racially balanced schools.

The project of school integration has always been challenging, and the results have been ambiguous at best. By the early 1970s, whites were in the minority in the cities of New York, Detroit, Chicago, Philadelphia, Cleveland and Washington, D.C. In some cities, efforts at overcoming this substantial racial residential imbalance have met forceful opposition. In 1974, Detroit attempted to improve racial balance in schools by establishing "metropolitan" school districts to incorporate portions of inner city Detroit with predominantly white sub-urban school districts. In a 5 to 4 decision, the move was declared unconstitutional by the U.S. Supreme Court (*Milliken v. Bradley*, 1974).

Those favoring school integration were dealt another blow by James S. Coleman, the author of the 1966 report on *Equality of Educational Opportunity*. In a 1975 report, he concluded that a court-imposed remedy to achieve school integration was encouraging "white flight," the movement of whites out of urban areas, and so were, in effect, self-defeating. The new Coleman study was roundly criticized by those who supported school integration as an intrinsic good. They were supported by those who feared that the remedy (e.g., busing) for segregated schools was more dangerous than the disease.

In a report prepared in 1984 to commemorate 30 years of the *Brown* decision, the authors, Braddock, Crain and McPartland, held, "The evidence already in hand tells us that the initial conception of the impact of school desegregation . . . has been borne out. The schools are the place in which society socializes its next generation of citizens. The research findings . . . suggest that the U.S. cannot afford segregated schools, if this nation is genuinely committed to provide equality of opportunity to every citizen."[9]

But as the 20th century comes to a close, Americans must still ask if the schools can become integrated in a society where large pockets of segregation still exist. Moreover, blacks themselves have begun to question the merits of school integration in favor of exercising a greater degree of control over their own schools.

Writing in 1967, Charles Silberman commented, ". . . the Coleman report suggests forcibly that the public schools do not—and as now constituted cannot—fulfill what has always been considered to be one of their main purposes and justifications: to ensure equality of opportunity . . . or, in Horace Mann's phrase, to be 'the balance wheel of the social machinery.'"[10]

While schools have yet to be thoroughly integrated, additional measures are also being considered to improve education for minority children. Integration can still be achieved, and efforts to attain integration must be pursued aggressively. The concept of the common school continues to embrace an ever larger number of children heretofore neglected.

Bilingual Education

Bilingual education, a means for the public schools to recognize and accommodate the cultural and language differences of minority groups, has been a much-debated issue. Much of this debate has revolved around racism and its effect on the education of many minority groups.

Racism is the belief that one group with seemingly common physical characteristics is superior to another. Black Americans, Native Americans, Hispanics, Asians and many groups have felt the sting of prejudice at one time or another.

The common schools attempted to fulfill their promise of providing an education for all. Yet, with increasing immigration, they were faced with the difficulty of educating a diverse national culture. Each group had its own rich traditions, often misunderstood by one another, as well as educators. Effective communication was difficult. Despite the goals identified in the Declaration of Independence: a "self-evident truth" that "all men are created equal," racism has been an important, if shameful, aspect of American life. Perhaps nowhere are the more insidious aspects of racism evident than in the public schools.

Bilingual education was a response to the growing awareness that the common school was not meeting its objectives of reaching out to all the children of America, especially to minorities who did not speak English as their first language.

In the 1950s, large numbers of immigrants began to arrive in America from the Caribbean, Central and South America and

Canada. Their arrival coincided with the great civil rights movements of those years. If blacks were right in demanding "black power," were not Native Americans, Hispanics and Asians likewise entitled to empowerment? In the process of seeking it out, these groups demanded that separate classroom studies of the origins and traditions of blacks, Native Americans, Hispanics and Asians be incorporated into the curriculum so young Americans could learn something of their diverse roots and take pride in them.

Immigrant groups urged that their children be taught in their native language so they would not fall behind their peers simply because they could not speak English. After considerable debate, Congress passed the Bilingual Education Act of 1968. It provided funds for local school districts to meet the needs of all children with limited capacity in the English language. Right from the start, however, there was much confusion as to what bilingualism really meant. On one hand, it was a means for children whose native language was not English to keep up with English-speaking children. Yet, bilingual education, more broadly defined, was also viewed as a means of making sure that children from minority groups were taught about their cultural heritage. Those in Congress adopted the first definition and thought of the new program mainly as a bridge for children who spoke Spanish or some other language. They would, for a time, be taught academic subjects in their native tongues until they possessed a sufficient mastery of English to join the mainstream of English-speaking children.

Bilingual educators, and the pressure groups who had lobbied in behalf of bilingual education, were also concerned about cultural heritage. They took advantage of the legislation to develop ethnic-awareness programs designed to sustain the new immigrants in their original culture. The Americanization of the immigrant, so much a part of the education of turn-of-the-century immigrants from Europe, became much less desired. Ethnic pride became increasingly important. The debate stirred up the education community; the conflict has never been completely resolved. If America is to be a pluralistic society, it should be able and willing to respect the ethnic traditions of immigrants while incorporating them into the larger society. Americanization need not mean the rejection of the traditions that children bring with them to the common school. But how best to encourage English-speaking proficiency without erasing the native languages of immigrants? We are still at work to find an answer.

In 1974, the U.S. Supreme Court decision in the case of *Lau v. Nichols* promoted bilingual, bicultural education by requiring public schools to provide for all children of limited English-speaking ability. A task force appointed by Terrell Bell, then secretary of education, insisted that all non-English-speaking children were to be taught in their native languages and were to study their native cultures. In 1977, the U.S. Office of Education reported that $115 million had been appropriated in more than 500 local districts to teach more than 300,000 children in their native languages. In addition, provision was made for the retraining of about 25,000 teachers and the preparation of teaching materials in 68 languages including Spanish, French, Korean, Chinese, Italian, Greek, Russian and Japanese, as well as seven Eskimo languages and a score of American Indian languages (some of which had no written form).[11]

Bilingualism retains a strong grip on American education despite the fact that objective research studies demonstrate "bilingual programs are neither better nor worse than other instructional methods . . . At the world level, the field of research on bilingual education is characterized by disparate findings and inconclusive results."[12] Under President Ronald Reagan, Secretary of Education William J. Bennett was skeptical about bilingual education and believed the programs to be ill-conceived and ineffectual.

In 1988, a revised bilingual education act allowed 25% of the bilingual-education budget to be spent on alternatives to teaching children in their native languages. Rita Esquivel, who was appointed to take charge of bilingual programs in the Department of Education, declares, "We on the federal level like to leave it up to the districts to decide on their particular program. But we certainly would like them to maintain their native languages. That's the President's point of view."[13]

In many ways, schools function as a global community. Bilingualism and the acceptance of multiculturalism move American schools in a direction less narrow-minded in character. An outreach of the common school is designed to help associate pluralism with Americanization, so that America's children understand it is possible to be a part of a racial, ethnic or national group and still be an American in every sense of the word.

Head Start

The Head Start program may be thought of as a further extension of the common school, by reaching kindergarten and pre-kindergarten children (between four and five years of age). In a sense, it may be thought of as an approach to the education of children that acknowledges the needs of today's families. From an educational standpoint, Head Start was viewed as an effort to give poor children a "head start" in life, enabling them to succeed and to keep up academically with their age group when they entered first grade. Established under the Economic Opportunity Act of 1964, Head Start enrolled half a million children in the summer of 1965, and between 1967 and 1970, 200,000 and 300,000 were enrolled annually in full-year programs.

Research on Head Start generally confirms the importance of providing academic stimulation to the very young. The

High/Scope Education Research Foundation of Ypsilanti, Michigan, found that the benefits of early childhood intervention programs, such as Head Start, had a direct impact on a child's future success. This success was measured in terms of the pursuit of further schooling and obtaining and holding a job.

Despite the obvious achievements of Head Start, efforts to expand the program faltered. Some legislators were concerned about costs; others feared Head Start would lead to the erosion of families by taking children out of the home too soon and placing them in school at a tender age. Despite these objections, however, in 1990 the 101st Congress made it possible for 40% of poor children to take part in Head Start. The legislation authorized enough funds so that by 1994, every eligible child will be able to participate.

Educating the Handicapped

The physically and mentally handicapped have historically had limited access to education. In that respect the handicapped have suffered educational deprivations similar to those of racial minority groups. Federal legislation has sought to correct that inequity. It has mandated that the schools take into account the special needs of the handicapped and develop programs to assure that they, too, have an opportunity to be educated.

The needs of the handicapped were recognized at the end of the 19th century, when the National Education Association had a separate department for the education of the handicapped. The definition of *handicapped* is a multifaceted one that includes both those who are mentally limited and those who are physically restricted in some way. More recently, Congress passed the Rehabilitation Act of 1973 to provide for the needs of the handicapped. At that time, it was estimated that between 5 to 8 million children were handicapped in one way or another.

There are two major questions involving the education of the handicapped: Is it better to educate the handicapped in a homogeneous setting, that is, to teach them along with other children who have similar disabilities? Or, should the handicapped be incorporated into the mainstream of the school and be taught alongside nonhandicapped children? During the early years of the common school, the educational decision-makers answered "yes" to the former question. Now a strong preference for "mainstreaming" is recognized.

In the Rehabilitation Act of 1973, the handicapped were assured that they could not be "... excluded from participation in, be denied the benefits of, or be subjected to discrimination under any program or activity receiving Federal financial assistance." The act was passed over President Nixon's veto with the assistance of a powerful lobby and help from the Bureau of Education for the Handicapped, a division of the Office of Education in 1966.

Legislation for the education of the handicapped was strengthened in 1975 with the passage of Public Law 94–142, entitled the "Education for All Handicapped Children Act." The law insisted that handicapped children be educated in "the least restrictive environment," thereby endorsing mainstreaming as the only acceptable way to educate the handicapped.

Although the financial burden the law placed on school districts was enormous, nearly all children with handicaps can now expect schools to offer some form of special education to meet their needs. In 1987– 88, 4,446,000 young people, from infancy to 21 years of age, were in federally supported special education programs with more than 70% being taught with their nonhandicapped schoolmates.[14]

The recurring "crises" in public education may be viewed as evidence of the common school's movement to achieve its laudatory goals. We have made great progress in expanding the vision of the common school as the provider of an education for *all*. This progress is shown by special programs to accommodate the needs of minority groups, non-English-speaking people, those from impoverished backgrounds and the physically and mentally handicapped. There is still much to be accomplished, but for the momentum to continue, schools must continually address the question: "Who should be taught?"

Schools must also answer the questions: "What should be taught?"; "How should it be taught?"; and "What standards of achievement are appropriate?" It is to these difficult issues that we must turn next.

Notes

Citations in the notes are brief. Full citations appear in the bibliography.

CHAPTER FOUR

1. Snyder, 103.
2. Greer, 29.
3. Silberman, 1971, 81.
4. Covello.
5. Ravitch, 3–5.
6. Myrdal, 416.
7. *The New York Times*, February 10, 1970.
8. Ravitch, 167.
9. Braddock II, Crain and McPartland, 259–264.
10. Silberman, in *Fortune* magazine, August, 1967, 181.
11. U.S. Congress, House Subcommittee on Elementary, Secondary, and Vocational Education of the Committee on Education and Labor, 71–81.
12. Ravitch, 279.
13. Bernstein, 48.
14. Snyder, 79–80.

CHAPTER FIVE

What Should Be Taught?

It is often said that war is too important a subject to be left only to soldiers. This is also true of education: Decisions about schools should not be left only to educators. It is not surprising that educators, parents, corporate executives and professionals in a host of fields are taking part in the continuing dialogue on what constitutes a good education.

If representatives of these groups were to participate in debates on the subject of education, there would be as many opinions as debaters. These differences would begin with confusion over words such as *real, good* and *knowledge*. For example: What is the role of education in preparing children to live in the *real* world? (What is the *real* world?) What is the obligation to provide all children with a *good* education? (What does a *good* education mean?) Should the goal of schools be to provide *knowledge* to students? (What is *knowledge*?)

Decisions about the complicated question of "What should be taught?" are deeply rooted in our understanding of "What is real?"; "What is good?"; "What is knowledge?" The following scenarios illustrate the issues at stake.[1]

What Is Real?

At the dinner table, one of your parents criticizes the schools for failing to prepare children for the "real" world. But what is real? The table you are sitting at is "real" enough, but it differs from the table you sit at when you have lunch in school and from the table on which you do your chemistry experiments.

Despite these differences, you, your parents and others can agree on what a table is because you recognize that *table* is only a name for objects that have certain things in common. To the scientist, a table is made up of molecules; to the artist, it is an object whose contours may be beautiful and symbolic; to the carpenter, it is the place at which he or she works. In fact, the "real" table, the table that makes it possible for a group of people to understand what is being talked about when the word *table* is used, is not at all the one at which you may be sitting but is one that does not exist at all. It exists only as an idea and not as a reality.

What does it mean to say that schools must educate for the "real" world? You experience the world in your own unique way, based on your daily life—the people you associate with, your race, your sex, your religion, your geographical location—and the ideas you value. Is one person's world more real than another's? Should educators decide on one definition for the "real" world, such as the world of work, and educate every student to live a certain way? These are tough questions.

What Is Good?

You are walking home from school with your best friend, and your friend starts telling you about a favorite rock band's new recording, describing it as "really good," and says that the two of you could stop at a local music store where, "you can get a good deal on it this week." But should you stop there now? You say, "I need to get home to start on a project that's due tomorrow.

I don't think taking time to go to buy a CD would be a good idea." Your friend says, "You have a point. I really shouldn't go either. I've decided that regular exercise would be good for me and I signed up for an aerobics class that starts tonight."

In each of these cases, the term *good* is used in a different sense. In the first, it refers to your friend's opinion that the new rock recording is of high quality. In the second, good is used to mean economical, meaning that the CD is priced reasonably. In the third, good refers to behavior or conduct: Those in authority—teachers and parents—dictate that the project be completed on time. In the last case, although the exercise interferes with what seems like more fun at the moment—stopping by the music store—your friend knows that the exercise would be valuable in promoting health.

When we apply the term *good* to education, do we mean the last example, one that may not be the most fun, but is "good" for the learner, or do we mean "good," as in the first example, based on one interpretation of quality? Or do we mean economical? You and your peers, your parents and teachers and your community may differ in their approaches to your education because each group has a different concept of what is "good."

What Is Knowledge?

You are ice skating across a frozen pond on a cold day in February. A friend comes by and asks if the ice is safe. You answer, "I know it is, because I've been skating all over it for the past 20 minutes." As you skate along, you and your friend talk about a movie that you have both seen, and you ask, "Did you know who the thief was before the ending?" Your friend replies, "I sure did. He just had that look." As you remove your skates, you say, "I guess I'll head for the library. I need to find out if Congress controls interstate commerce for a paper I'm writing." Your friend replies, "I know it does. It's in the U.S. Constitution."

In each of these cases, the word *know* is used in a different sense. In the first case, the ice is known to be safe because it is tested through experience, that is, skating over it. In the second case, knowing is intuitive; no one looks like a thief, but the viewer had some intuitive insight about the character in the movie chosen as the thief. The third use of knowing is based on authority; it is in the Constitution. As these cases illustrate, the words *knowing* and *knowledge* mean rather different things at different times. When there is debate about what should be taught in school, that debate largely grows out of differences among people concerning what is meant by *knowledge* and what it means to *know*.

Three schools of thought have different ideas about what should be taught in schools based on differences in the approach to reality, goodness and knowledge. These schools of thought are *perennialism, essentialism* and *progressivism*. Each of these will be described, the first two in brief, while progressivism, because it has had a profound effect on modern education, will be explored in more depth. Other key issues, including the teaching of reading and the role of religion, will also be discussed.

Perennialism

The word *perennial* means "everlasting." As the term implies, perennialist educators believe children and young adults should be taught only everlasting or enduring truths. Perennialists believe these truths may be found in a limited number of great books, written by a few brilliant people over the course of humanity. To the perennialist, once students have mastered the basics, anything else is a waste of time since these great truths have been tested and have remained eternal verities throughout the generations and for all cultures. Perennialists view these truths as the only permanent realities.

Thus, according to the perennialist, schools should concentrate on teaching Socrates, Plato and Aristotle and other elements of our classical (Greek and Roman) heritage, as well as the literary and philosophical works of the European Middle Ages (approximately 500–1400) and the Renaissance (approximately 1500–1700). Of course, even among perennialists, there is disagreement as to which books are "great." Some schools with a "great books" approach include in their programs more recent great books, which were written after the Renaissance. Perennialists believe we have failed to apply the eternal principles of great authors and philosophers to the scientific and technological developments of our own time.

Among educators of the perennialist school of thought are Robert Hutchins (1899–1977), former president of the University of Chicago, and his colleague, the philosopher Mortimer Adler (born in 1902), both of whom wrote extensively throughout their lengthy careers. Through a study of the great works of the past, Hutchins and Adler believed that young people would become acquainted with the eternal concerns that face humankind through the ages. These concerns include acting justly, living peaceably, pursuing truth, understanding beauty, living honorably, acting courageously and governing fairly. Instead of learning from textbooks, Hutchins and Adler identified approximately 100 great books that they considered the only ones worth studying in detail after basic skills were acquired. Originally confined to the great literature of Western culture, great works of other cultures have recently been included as well.

While perennialists may deny it, their approach to education can be described as elitist. Perennialism implies that there are wise people who are capable of identifying the eternal truths about which there can be no disagreement. In this respect, perennialism can be compared to Thomas Jefferson's views on education, as discussed in Chapter Two. Jefferson, who was also accused of being elitist, viewed the school as a place where the "natural aristocracy" of talent was identified. Perennialism appears to clash with democracy, a philosophy of politics that states no one authority is capable of dictating which "truths" should be taught to the youth. Who has the authority to determine the "real" truths and to impose these truths on others?

Sensitive to the criticisms that perennialist views were elitist, Mortimer Adler and his colleagues developed *The Padeia Proposal* in 1982. This proposal criticized most modern educational practices as too career-oriented in focus. The proposal called for a renewal of academics and a spread of general learning through the study of great works and classics. The objectives of education would be universal; namely, (1) mental, moral and spiritual self-improvement; (2) adequate preparation for discharging the duties and responsibilities of citizenship; (3) preparation in the basic skills common to all work. Schooling must take account of the adult's need to earn a living, but schools should not prepare students only for a specific task.[2]

Schools would be organized in a nonvocational, one-track system with no electives. Teaching would combine lectures and Socratic techniques, using questions to encourage logical thought patterns necessary to reach ultimate conclusions. Adler argued that his proposal would produce the enlightened citizens a democratic society needs—a generation of free thinkers—and that education would be restored to its preeminent role in society.

Essentialism

Essentialists believe it is the function of the school to transmit the essential cultural heritage to learners by whatever means are available to educators. The essentials of any education are based upon traditional academic disciplines such as history, geography, math and science. These subjects are modified by teachers to take into account the age level, educational background and intelligence of the children being taught.

To the essentialist, mastery of basic knowledge and skills is a must. The teacher might try to make the subject matter more interesting, but at the same time it is important to avoid making the learning process too easy because this would do a disservice to the learner whose mind must be engaged. In other words, essentialists believe that the learning process should be a continuous challenge. To this end, essentialists use time-honored practices—the frequent testing of students to evaluate how much has been learned, the use of textbooks to draw the essentials of a subject together in an orderly sequence, and the evaluation of students by grades on a numerical or letter basis.

"Building character," "mastery of subject matter," and "intellectual training" are among the phrases commonly associated with the essentialist view. Among practices endorsed or encouraged by essentialists is the emphasis on memorization of names, dates, places, people and important inspirational works of literature. Equally important is the technique of rote learning and oral drills to encourage mastery and instant response.

Moreover, essentialists believe schools must encourage devotion to the nation, the acceptance of its traditions and a reverence for its past. To the essentialist, knowledge does not change very much, at least in terms of the essentials needed to succeed in life.

More than most other educational philosophies, essentialism draws on many sources and a variety of teaching methods to systematize knowledge and to teach it to the young methodically. To the essentialist, "reality" is in the here and now as science, technology and social science make evident. Essentialist education is closely related to current, practical situations and deals with contemporary issues of law, order and custom. Among 20th-century essentialists are William C. Bagley (1874–1946), as well as Herman C. Horne (1874–1946), who said, "Truth is the agreement of statement with fact . . ."[3] Essentialists believe that it is the task of the teacher to choose selected aspects of facts, laws, practices, customs and achievements and to plan instruction so as to bring about effective learning.

Progressivism

In recent years, progressivism, or "progressive education," has fallen out of favor with most educators. Progressive education has come to be blamed for many of the faults that American society has found with its schools. Yet, as noted earlier, progressivism may be thought of as America's distinctive contribution to education.

Rooted in faith in democracy, progressive educators believe in the following:

1. Learning should be experienced, that is, it should be active rather than passive, and should be cooperatively planned by pupils and teachers.
2. Sensitivity to the needs of the group should replace those of the individual; and cooperative effort should replace individual competition for grades.
3. Cooperation should not ignore individual differences. On the contrary, cooperation requires that such differences be taken into account. The curriculum of the school should encourage self-expression by allowing students to develop their strengths and talents in reading, music, art, science, mathematics, or in any other way. Educational "growth" is more important than mastery of subject matter.
4. Because facts sometimes change radically, "knowing"

facts by rote memorization should be replaced by learning to live effectively in a rapidly changing environment.

5. Traditional subjects should merge in a core curriculum based on topics such as family life, community living, the nature of work and the best uses of leisure time.

6. In teaching these subjects, teachers should not rely merely on books but use many sources of information, including popular ones, and provide as many appropriate experiences as possible.

7. Cooperation among children should be encouraged in the form of a variety of group activities and assignments.

8. Because children would be living as adults in a democratic society, the classroom should provide experiences in living and learning democratically. The teacher should no longer be the central authority figure in the room; the teacher and pupils should work together to plan learning activities. Progressive educators use the word *socialization* as a synonym for the group activities they prefer.

9. Recognizing that a larger number of children who enter school would not go on to higher education, progressive educators urge that non-college-bound students be given as much attention as those planning to go to college.

10. Progressive educators tend to focus on the present and the future rather than on the past, on solving problems rather than memorizing facts, on learning by sharing experiences rather than by taking notes on teachers' lectures.

While its roots go back to the 1890s, progressivism has been the dominant philosophy of American education at least since the end of World War II in 1945. It has had the support of many of the nation's best philosophical minds and has influenced education from nursery schools to colleges. Although that influence is no longer as pervasive as it once was, important aspects of progressive education remain with us to this day and are unlikely to be abandoned.

Progressive education was rooted in what historians call the Progressive Era of American history, roughly from 1890 to 1914. Believing that drastic domestic reform was needed to make American society more just, battles were fought against the so-called malefactors of great wealth, financial tycoons like J. P. Morgan in banking, John D. Rockefeller in oil, or Cornelius Vanderbilt in railroads. Writers of the Progressive Era who sought to expose corruption, inefficiency and abuses were called "muckrakers" because of the "muck," or dirt, they raked up. The Progressive Era's spirit of reform was not limited to business and government; other institutions, including education, were also examined.

Among the muckrakers was a young doctor named Joseph Mayer Rice (1857–1934), who may be thought of as the "father of Progressive Education." Dr. Rice took an interest in pedagogy (the science of teaching) and immersed himself thoroughly in the philosophical and spiritual aspects of teaching. He studied in the German universities at Jena and Leipzig and went on to examine education in the United States. He visited 36 American cities from Boston to Washington, from New York to St. Louis, interviewed 1,200 teachers and visited 20 teacher-training institutions. He interviewed parents and attended an endless number of school board meetings. Rice was determined, in his words, ". . . to place no reliance whatever on reports published by school officials regarding the condition of their schools. . . . I relied . . . only on personal observation of classroom instruction."[4]

What he observed distressed him.

In a series of articles published in the popular journal *Forum* and later as a book in 1893, Dr. Rice established himself as a "muckraker for education," roundly criticizing the "mechanical" teaching he found and the "damp and chilly" atmosphere this teaching encouraged. Incompetent, authoritarian teachers were common, as illustrated by the teacher in a classroom in New York City who demanded of her pupils, "Don't stop to think; tell me what you know!" Rice also uncovered rampant corruption in the schools, with teaching jobs being awarded on the basis of political favoritism rather than the teachers' ability.

Yet, he found some good teaching methods, calling them "progressive." In Indianapolis, for example, he observed a teacher asking the children in her classroom to tell and then write a story. As Rice reports: "A little boy is much amused before breakfast by seeing his cat jump over a stick. Soon after this occasion he goes to school. The teacher instructs in reading by the sentence method. During the reading lesson she calls on the children for little stories, and as they are given she writes them upon the board for reading matter. When our little boy tells his story, he says, 'My cat kin jump.' The teacher remarks 'My cat can jump,' and writes this on the board. When the reading lesson is over, each child is told to write his own story upon his slate. The little boy sets to work and draws the words of his story as he sees them on the board. He is happy to find that he has the ability to write a story about his cat, and he thinks school is a jolly place because it has something to do with his cat."[5]

Dr. Rice found other, but still too rare, examples of teachers who understood the needs of children, who were aware of what interested them, and had the patience and ability to encourage their talents. Where he found such teachers, Rice witnessed "a truly progressive spirit, much enthusiasm, and a desire to become conversant with the laws of psychology and principles of education."[6] Think back to the 10 basic beliefs of progressive education listed earlier in this section. What came to be later called "progressive education," was, in part, a response to the shortcomings in the nation's schools that writers like Rice and others observed as widespread.

Progressive educators encouraged schools to take on the task of turning boys and girls into better men and women. That schools could successfully achieve such a result was part of the optimism of the progressive philosophy. In the attempt to improve individual lives, schools were encouraged to become concerned with the health of the child, the family and the community in which he or she lived—and the manner in which he or she might eventually make a living. Moreover, since progressive educators also valued scientific progress, they strived to apply the latest scientific developments to improve teaching. This meant drawing heavily upon the new science of psychology, including intelligence testing to find out the intelligence quotient (IQ) of an individual, or aptitude testing to identify a child's potential talents. The use of intelligence tests in schools began in the 1920s and increased rapidly in the decades that followed. By using the results of such tests, children were to be "tracked," that is, placed in groups and taught according to their ability.

Progressive educators did not believe that training in one subject area could automatically be transferred to another. For example, they felt that teaching mathematics was not also necessarily "training the mind" to think logically, it was merely teaching mathematics. According to some progressive educators, all subject matter was equally valid in contributing to mental development. With this conviction, progressive educators denied that some subjects were better than others. Once students learned the basic skills, no subject needed to be required of all students.

John Dewey (1859–1952), who taught in the philosophy department of Columbia University, was the philosophical giant of progressive education, and his classic work, *Democracy and Education* (1916), remains an influential treatise on education as well as philosophy. Since what he wrote was difficult to read, both in terms of its content and writing style, most educators derived what they knew from the writings and oversimplifications of others. Unfortunately, it was not long before progressive educators undercut the very philosophy they were themselves preaching. Dewey lived long enough to try to correct the widespread misinterpretation of his views and to distance himself from the corruption of his philosophy at the hands of educators who did not read his work and rarely understood his theories.

Among progressive educators, the phrase, "We teach children, not subjects," was common. They thought they were following a progressivist approach, based on their rather distorted view of what Dewey had in mind. Dewey understood the need for a balance between stimulating the desire to learn and focusing on the subject matter; many of his followers believed that what was taught was less important than a recognition of the character of the child and the environment from which he or she came. This meant freely tailoring instruction to the needs of the child, even compromising the subject matter to keep education "fun."

By the early 1950s, progressive education reached its peak. By then, most teachers were trained by teachers' colleges to be "progressive" educators. The curricula of nearly all school districts were revised so as to reflect the principles of progressive education; failure to do so could lead to denial of accreditation (approval) from the various state departments of education. Among the major innovations were programs collectively labeled "life adjustment education."

"Life adjustment" was never clearly defined, even by progressive educators. But in effect, it replaced some traditional academic disciplines with courses that taught skills and knowledge designed to help youth better live as citizens, workers and family members. In a course on "Developing an Effective Personality," junior high school students in Tulsa, Oklahoma, were taught how to improve their appearance by learning the clothing, nail polish or hair style appropriate to them.[7] Schools were encouraged to develop courses in good health habits, community issues, leisure activities and on home and family life.

Progressive education became the prevailing conventional wisdom, that is, the agreed upon consensus among educators. However, its critics made their views known, too.

Attacks on Progressive Education

Parents gradually became aware of the shortcomings of progressive education, yet were also fearful of confronting educators who supposedly "knew" better. With the progressive approach, students were given a wide variety of subjects to choose from, and classes in the "life adjustment" category were often conducted with small groups of students and required expensive supplies. Community members who questioned the value of these courses were called hard-hearted and accused of being indifferent to the proper education of the next generation. As a result, few were brave enough to stand up to progressive educators and the host of organizations and publications that supported them.

Gradually, by the year 1953, critics with enough authority to command the attention of the public were making their views known. They had the courage to say progressive education had become a sham, and their message could not be ignored. Robert Hutchins, a supporter of the perennial philosophy discussed earlier in this chapter, questioned whether students were getting the depth of education that they needed in school. In his book, *The Conflict in Education in a Democratic Society*, he wrote: "Perhaps the greatest idea that America has given the world is the idea of education for all. The world is entitled to know whether this idea means that everybody can be educated, or only that everybody must go to school."[8]

The most serious criticism of progressive education came from Arthur Bestor, a teacher and historian at the University of Illinois and former instructor at Teacher's College in New York.

As a youth, he had attended the Lincoln School of Columbia University's Teacher's College in New York, one of the most respected progressive schools in the country (no longer in existence). In his 1953 book, *Educational Wastelands*, he wrote: "The West was not settled by men and women who had taken courses in 'How to be a pioneer.'" He went on to assert that ". . . I for one do not believe that the American people have lost all common sense and native wit so that now they have to be taught in school to blow their noses and button their pants."[9]

Bestor openly condemned what he viewed as the failure of progressive education to teach the young how to think. He felt that to learn this, students needed basic education and the traditional academic disciplines—all of which was de-emphasized in progressive education. In his 1955 book, *The Restoration of Learning*, Bestor urged a return to the indispensable studies of reading, writing and arithmetic at the elementary school level. In the high school, he urged basic subjects such as math, science, history, English and American literature and foreign languages.

In 1957, when a Soviet rather than an American space satellite became the first to orbit the Earth, Americans were shocked, at least temporarily, out of their lethargy. More federal funds were demanded for education and more math and science requirements were urged upon the schools. The blame went to progressive education; it had failed to be responsive to the needs of the mid-20th century. While Sputnik alone did not cause the demise of progressive education, it symbolically established the fact that a more rigorous course of study was needed for the nation's youth. How could that be accomplished? Important debates over the proper subjects for students remain with us today.

Basic Education

Bestor's books mainly, but others as well, fueled a "back-to-basics" movement in American education during the 1950s.

This movement can be characterized as a response to the ongoing debate over the merits of education versus scholarship. Education can be defined as providing children with the basic knowledge and skills needed to function successfully in society. Scholarship can be defined as the excellence needed for in-depth understanding of one or more subjects. Traditionally, the American people have had a profound faith in education, and a profound suspicion of scholarship and those who are labeled as "scholars." This contradiction is the basis for the controversies about what should be taught in the public schools.

Those urging a return to basics believed that education and scholarship had been divorced from each other. They urged that what is taught to students at all levels needed to be rooted in the scholarly disciplines. This approach combines the essential and perennial philosophies of education.

The back-to-basics movement represents a significant attack on progressive education. The road map it offers, however, is unclear. For one thing, art, music and other aesthetic studies are absent from the curriculum. Are these eliminated because they are not "basic" or because of a desire to cut educational costs? Moreover, Bestor and his colleagues say little about what should be studied in history, science, English or any of the other subjects, and he says much less about how these subjects should be taught. Bestor's back-to-basics movement illustrates the concerns of those who proposed alternatives to the progressive movement; the movement also illustrates how difficult it is to progress from criticism to specific solutions. Cultural literacy, a recent development in education, is based on similar concerns as the back-to-basics movement. Cultural literacy goes a step further by prescribing the specific knowledge, in areas such as history, that students should gain in school.

Properly understood, progressive educators did not deny the value of these studies. But, in attempting to stimulate interest, they often failed to encourage students to do the hard work that academic disciplines demand. Moreover, progressive educators sought to adapt these courses for those of limited ability who could not possibly master them. Bestor, the major proponent of the back-to-basics approach, has little to say about the significant number of young people who cannot or will not learn very much from the traditional academic disciplines, yet educators cannot ignore this important group.

Reading

Since reading is so basic to education, it is not surprising that questions of how to teach it and how to measure reading levels and the success of teaching methods became a fundamental issue in the debate over the progressive versus the back-to-basics approach to education. While there are many issues, the conflict centers around whether teaching phonics or the "whole word" method is more effective. In his book, *Why Johnny Can't Read* (1955), Rudolf Flesch blamed the replacement of the phonics method with the whole word method for youth's reading problems.

Phonics is a method of teaching reading based on pronunciation. The sounds of letters or groups of letters provide clues about how a word is pronounced. Asking students to remember a group of similar-sounding words such as how, now, cow, or sat, hat, cat, bat is an example of phonics. Progressive educators held that the phonic approach essentially required memorization of nonsense syllables, or at best words, that children could memorize but not understand. Of what use was it, claimed critics of phonics, for an urban child to know *cow* if he or she had never seen one and did not know anything about the role of the cow in the world's food chain?

Opponents of phonics preferred the whole word method of instruction where a child learned a limited number of simple words that he or she fully understood, could recognize in a book and could also use in both reading and writing a short story. Many of the readers that children used in school were based on the whole word method of teaching and involved very simple stories about "Dick and Jane," to cite the title of the highly popular reading series. The Dick and Jane books gradually became more complex from the first through the sixth grades.

Progressive educators generally preferred the whole word method to teach reading and were successful in making it the dominant approach during the 1940s and early 1950s. Nevertheless, there was widespread fear that the reading level of America's youth was inadequate to the emergence of a highly complex society. Was the switch from phonics to the whole word approach the reason? While the evidence is not clear, the controversy continues. Increasingly, phonics is returning to the classroom. The general consensus appears to be that phonics (teaching reading by sound) and whole word approaches (teaching reading through actual experience of known words and associations) need to be combined. Deciding on the appropriate proportion of each remains a subject of inquiry and experimentation.

Religion

The First Amendment states: "Congress shall make no law respecting an establishment of religion, or prohibiting the free exercise thereof." What this amendment means in its application to public schooling has long been debated and continues to be a cause of curriculum controversy.

Thomas Jefferson believed the amendment meant there was "a wall of separation between church and state." But was he right? Was it a wall made of concrete, or was it a thin curtain through which church and state could at least feel each other's presence? "In God We Trust," is stamped on our coins, and

Congress opens its sessions with a prayer. Should the schools be expected to do less?

The teaching of evolution is a prime example of the controversy over the role of religion in the schools. In 1925, the state of Tennessee passed a law forbidding any public school from ". . . teaching the theory that denies the story of the divine creation of man (evolution) as taught in the Bible." To test the constitutionality of the law, John T. Scopes, a biology teacher from Dayton, Tennessee, taught that human beings evolved over long periods of time from other forms of life. This is the theory of evolution. Scopes was arrested and the trial that followed generated an enormous amount of publicity. The renowned lawyer Clarence Darrow (1857–1938) was the attorney for Scopes while William Jennings Bryan (1860–1925), a former presidential candidate, supported the state and presented himself as an authority on the Bible.

Scopes was convicted of breaking the law against the teaching of evolution. Although the Tennessee supreme court described the case as "bizarre," it upheld the conviction but set aside the sentence based on legal technicalities. The case's impact was widespread. Despite the conviction, the trial's circuslike atmosphere and the court's own description of the case as "bizarre" caused other states to delay their passing similar legislation under consideration.

Although the Scopes case took place more than 65 years ago, boards of education are still troubled over what to teach about evolution. This has an impact on both methods and materials of instruction. In less publicized cases, during the years that followed, the issue has taken the form of the theory of evolution as Charles Darwin developed it in 1859, and as scientists later refined it, versus what some call creationism, or the biblical account of the world's creation.

It is important to note that this controversy is centered around the teaching of the creationist point of view. The most narrow view of creation, which does not acknowledge the validity of alternate points of view, such as evolution, is held predominantly by religious fundamentalists, not by all religious people.

Nearly all scientists have accepted some form of biological evolution; many people who believe in God or who are agnostic (unsure of the existence of God) also accept the theory of evolution on some level. Some groups of religious fundamentalists feel that the theory of evolution denies the biblical account that God created all living things. Convinced of the legitimacy of their cause, those at the extreme of religious fundamentalism continue to believe that creationism belongs in school and have repeatedly attempted to get their viewpoint across by lobbying (using community influence) local school boards far from the glare of national publicity. In these efforts, they have met with at least partial success.

The teaching of creationism has not been generally accepted as a reasonable alternative to evolution. However, since the religiously devout are numerous, they can, and have, intimidated local school boards during the last two decades. To accomplish their goals in these cases, they used a variety of tactics: They kept their children home; they sometimes voted against funds for education, unless concessions to their point of view were made; and they conducted public and many times abrasive demonstrations. Through these tactics religious fundamentalists instilled enough fear in timid school boards, teachers and administrators and influenced publishers of science and social studies textbooks that in many schools the theory of evolution is taught superficially, if at all, even today.

It is hard to imagine a credible biology course that does not teach the theory of evolution. Though creationism is a matter of faith, creationists claim that evolution is "merely" a theory and should not be taught as a fact. In a way, of course, they are correct. In the realm of science, however, a theory has a powerful status and is not simply a guess or a provocative position taken by radical or alienated groups. Scientists distinguish between a hypothesis, or a hunch, and a theory. A scientific theory is based on evidence and is much more likely to be proven true in some form. Archaeological excavations have provided evidence for the theory of evolution.

When in the late 1960s a federally funded biological sciences curriculum study endorsed teaching the theory of evolution, creationists became alarmed and fought to get creationism (sometimes also called creation science) taught along with the theory of evolution. In 1968, in *Epperson v. Arkansas*, the Supreme Court held that the Arkansas state law forbidding public schools to teach evolution was unconstitutional. The basis for this decision came from the First and Fourteenth Amendments, forbidding ". . . the preference of a religious doctrine or the prohibition of a theory which is deemed antagonistic to a particular dogma . . . The State has no legitimate interest in protecting any or all religions from views distasteful to them." In 1987, the Supreme Court held that the teaching of creationism was a violation of the First Amendment which addresses the separation of church and state. Even now, many teachers and administrators are concerned about how best to teach evolution without confronting or offending the religious sensibilities of their students.

The Debate Over Religion

If the schools cannot teach religion, can they teach *about* religion and should they do so? How should religion and science be separated? On this point, interestingly enough, both politically liberal and religiously conservative groups deplore the fact that the role of religion in American life has not received the attention they feel it deserves. Even if everyone agrees that religion has a place in American public education, should it be introduced into such courses as history and/or literature?

Should there be separate courses in, for example, comparative religions where students explore the major beliefs of all religions? In either case, the objectivity of teachers and materials may be called into question, especially where the equally devout may have differing views.

Moreover, if teaching about religion is reasonable, which religions should be taught? Only the Western religions such as Judaism and Christianity? In a global society, how can the views of Islam, Hinduism, Buddhism and a host of other non-Western religions be ignored? How can they be objectively taught? How shall the views of atheists (those who believe in no religion at all) be respected?

In attempting to define what the authors of the First Amendment meant, the Supreme Court clearly addressed the role of the government in religious affairs in *Everson v. the Board of Education* (1947), which concerned the busing of children to parochial schools. In its decision on this case, discussed later in this section, the Court stated:

> Neither a state nor the Federal Government can set up a church. Neither can pass laws which aid one religion, aid all religions, or prefer one religion over another. Neither can force or influence a person to go to or to remain away from church against his will or force him to profess a belief or disbelief in any religion. No person can be punished for entertaining or professing religious beliefs or disbeliefs, for church attendance or nonattendance. No tax in any amount, large or small, can be levied to support any religious activities or institutions, whatever they may be called, or whatever form they may adopt to teach or practice religion. Neither a state nor the Federal Government can, openly or secretly, participate in the affairs of any religious organizations or groups and vice versa. In the words of Jefferson, the clause against establishment of religion by law was intended to erect "a wall of separation between church and state."

If the schools cannot teach a particular religion, should they open their doors to all religions? In the case of *McCollum v. the Board of Education* (1948), the Supreme Court held that religious instruction in schools for Catholic, Protestant and Jewish children was unconstitutional because the public schools must be neutral between belief and disbelief. Schools may not immerse themselves in religious affairs even if they treat all faiths equally. Freedom of choice comes first in a democratic society; it is difficult to teach religion from an objective viewpoint and without influencing students in the direction of one belief over another. Because of this concern, decisions about religion are best left outside school and to the discretion of parents.

There are really two separate concerns regarding the public schools and religion. Clearly, schools are not allowed to teach religion. Yet, can the state support religious education outside of the public schools?

Since the teaching of religion was not allowed in the schools, could children be released to obtain religious instruction outside of school, perhaps attending their church or synagogue for a portion of a school day? In *Zorach v. Clauson* (1952), the Supreme Court held that releasing children for religious instruction was constitutional, assuming that the public school did nothing more than adjust the schedules of those participating.

Could public schools provide textbooks, lunches and transportation for children attending parochial schools? In the 1930 case of *Cochran v. the Louisiana State Board of Education*, the Supreme Court ruled that since the children and not the religious denomination would benefit from the availability of textbooks at state expense, such provision was constitutional. This decision was confirmed in 1962 in the case of the *Board of Education v. Allen*. And in *Everson v. the Board of Education* (1947), the Supreme Court held in a 5 to 4 decision that a state could constitutionally finance bus transportation to children attending religious as well as public schools.

Prayer in the public schools has also been questioned and debated in the courts. A nondenominational prayer written by the New York State Board of Regents to be read aloud each morning was declared unconstitutional by the Supreme Court of the United States in the case of *Engle v. Vitale* (1962). The Court ruled that "In this country, it is no part of the business of government to compose official prayers for any group of the American people to recite as part of a religious program carried on by government."

Selected Curriculum Controversies

Today, there is no single dominating educational philosophy. Perhaps, because there is none, curriculum controversy is seemingly unending. What is basic education and how can it be encouraged? What is the most effective way to teach reading? What place, if any, does religion have in public schools?

The term *curriculum* is derived from the Latin word *currere*, which means to run. More specifically, curriculum means a course that has to be completed in order to achieve a specific objective, that is, a diploma or degree. Curriculum may be defined as the classes and experiences that schools provide students in the process of educating them.

With this definition in mind, curriculum includes not only the courses of study, but all the activities associated with school, including athletics, clubs, drama, band, orchestra, dances, student newspaper, student government, yearbook, assemblies, awards and graduation proceedings. Some of these activities are referred to as extracurricular, since they often take place after the school day. All are designed to enhance learning, so the distinction is not essential. Nearly every aspect of these activities, however, has been the subject of controversy, and a number of selected issues are discussed in the following text.

Those who debate the issue of what should be taught in schools are students, their parents, teachers and administrators, and the community as represented by lawmakers, special-interest groups and adults who have no children currently in school. While these groups agree on many things, there are still differences that often make communication difficult. These differences, however minor, tend to worsen curriculum controversies.

By way of example, in 1984, John Goodlad, the distinguished educator, asked junior and senior high school students, "What is the *one* best thing about this school?" It should surprise no one when the students answered, "my friends," "sports," and "good student attitudes," in that order. In the junior high school, 62% collectively felt this way, as did 58% of the junior and senior high school students. Furthermore, "nothing" was the response of 8% of the junior and senior high school students, even outranking, "classes I am taking" (7%). "Teachers" were hardly ever the best thing about school: Only 5% at the junior high school level and 3% at the senior high school level gave this response.[10] Educators understand that relationships with friends seem more important to students than academics do, yet it is difficult to take this into account effectively when developing school curricula.

As for parents, the Goodlad study revealed that discipline and drug and alcohol abuse were high among their concerns. Substantially less concern for the quality of teachers and of programs was evidenced, and even less with the administration of the school or curriculum. Instead, parents are concerned about what may be called the custodial side of education. This has to do with an understandable desire to be sure their children are in a safe, caring and nurturing environment. Interestingly enough, however, it is when parental concern over safety reaches a critical point that dissatisfaction with the school mounts. Cries for more discipline and back-to-basic studies grow stronger. Educational "frills" are scorned.

Teachers and parents both share concern for drug and alcohol abuse, and likewise desire a nurturing environment for children, but teachers have a different view of their role as educators than do parents. Goodlad wrote that "Research ... portrays teachers as believing that it takes a teacher to stimulate intellectual curiosity and interest in school."[11] Teachers believe themselves to be vital primarily to the intellectual role of the school, with limited power to change the environment of the schools and their curricula. Yet at the same time, school principals believe teachers have a great deal of power to make changes.

Beyond Progressivism

While its formal organization, the Progressive Education Association, died in 1955, and its journal, *Progressive Education*, ended publication in 1957, progressive education deserves to be remembered for two major reasons. First, much of what it stood for remains in the public schools to this day. Second, naive though it may have been, progressive education was a specific and hopeful response to the shortcomings of the public schools as they were then perceived.

Progressive education no longer dominates the educational enterprise. Yet, we still live within its shadows. Good teachers still provide for individual differences. Excessive reliance on rote responses continue to be shunned. Children still work and play in groups. They continue to be engaged in projects to benefit the community and foster good citizenship.

Today's responses to concerns about the public schools are often marked by pessimism rather than optimism as people look for solutions. Do we need more religious influence in our schools? Do we need a return to the basic disciplines? Should we renew the pursuit of higher academic standards? Do we need to take another look at the qualifications of teachers?

What about the issue of "Who should teach?" This question has been debated throughout the history of education. As you will see in the next chapter, the debate continues.

Notes

Citations in the notes are brief. Full citations appear in the bibliography.

CHAPTER FIVE

1. Brameld, 38–40.
2. Adler, 16–17.
3. Horne, 500.
4. Rice, 2.
5. Ibid., 23.
6. Ibid., 115.
7. Ravitch, 69.
8. Hutchins, 54.
9. Bestor, 64.
10. Goodlad, 77.
11. Ibid.

C H A P T E R   S I X

Who Should Teach?

"**W**ho should teach?" is a broad question. The most obvious answer is, "Teachers!" Yet the definition of a teacher is being questioned. Teacher certification and competency concerns are being raised. Job satisfaction has become an issue. Teachers are demanding better working conditions and higher pay and have organized themselves to collectively bargain with school districts to attain their demands.

Other related issues also come into play in answering, "Who should teach?" In our age of technology, we can tap into our imaginations to take the "who" of the question beyond human beings. Technology is playing an increasing role in our daily lives, yet television and computers have had minimal impact on the classroom. Educators are taking a close look at the potential uses for technology in education.

We also need to look past the walls of the public school, and examine whether students and parents need more flexibility to make their own decisions about who will do the teaching. Freedom of choice might mean taking a portion of money allotted for an individual student's public education and allowing him or her to spend it on the public or private school of choice. But are students and parents qualified to decide which schools are "good"?

While asking, "Who should teach?" has led to much debate, it has also led to action as when concerned citizens in Chicago took matters into their own hands. In 1984, the Alliance for Better Chicago Schools (ABC) decided to fight back against what it called a "disaster of a school system." The alliance, an organization made up predominantly of concerned parents, demanded massive reorganization in the city's school administration, beginning at the top. The group called upon the city's new school superintendent to fire the top 100 administrators and to recruit new administrators in open competition.

The ABC did not stop there. It announced plans to make a clean sweep of the Chicago schools. The group reviewed the way teachers are trained and how they are appointed and examined how Chicago schools are funded. This knowledge gave them the clout to make changes in the way Chicago schools are organized. The alliance was determined to make a difference in the way large urban schools address their seemingly unsolvable problems.

Given the challenges that American society faces, citizens have serious concerns about the ability of our institutions—especially our schools—to deal with these challenges. It is not surprising that our schools are in turmoil. What *is* surprising is that, despite the upheaval in society, as well as a host of major school reform proposals designed to address them, the fundamental structure and organization of schools themselves has changed very little. The 20th century has been one of progress, but the schools have in many ways stayed on the sidelines.

School and Society

In a story by Washington Irving, Rip Van Winkle falls asleep for 20 years. When he awakens, he finds his community substantially changed. If a modern Rip Van Winkle had fallen asleep, say, in 1940, and awakened 50 years later in 1990 to return to the schools he attended, he would find that while there have been some changes in the schools, they would look and function about the same as they always have. Students would still be spending the school day by going from class to class in, most likely, the same, possibly remodeled, school building. Even though society is radically different from what it was 50 years ago, by and large, the schools would be more recognizable than one would expect.

The approximately 180-day school year and six-hour-and-20-minute school day is a remnant of an agrarian economy when children were expected to work on the family farm. This school schedule remains in place.

While there are some new buildings, there are also many old ones, especially in the inner cities of large metropolitan areas. Too many of these buildings are covered with graffiti, need fundamental repair, and offer an environment that is not always comfortable or conducive to learning. While many of the new buildings are air-conditioned, too many are not, making them difficult to use in the summer.

Although children's desks are no longer screwed to the floor, they are still mainly aligned in rows. All eyes face front where the teacher is likely to stand. The blackboard, now called a chalkboard because it might be blue or green, still dominates the classroom.

Perhaps most remarkable is the absence of educational technology, including television, computers and projectors of various kinds. Although they are often available in substantial numbers, this equipment is not as essential to education as in agriculture or industry. Instead, the advancements seem to be perceived as "add-ons" or frills that have made little difference in the delivery of education. Many teachers are still unprepared, or unskilled, to use them and administrators have not given adequate attention to their maintenance. Teachers suffer from the same lingering fear of computers as people in business and industry. Often, for want of a simple piece of equipment, like a cable, the computer cannot be used and the lesson is lost. Textbooks—bigger and more profusely illustrated—remain important instructional tools, while the school library, all too often, remains under-used. It is easier to pick up a textbook than it is to take the time and energy to explore the library. Yet, our modern-day Rip Van Winkle would find that the library still comes into the limelight when parents object to books their children find there. J. D. Salinger's *Catcher in the Rye*, with its alleged profanity, is often on the "hit list" of school library book purgers.

Rip Van Winkle would also see that books dealing with sex still raise a community's collective eyebrow, just as they did in 1940; while some parents and school board members are more tolerant than others, the subject still generates disagreement. What schools should do about sex education remains a controversial topic in most communities. Yet, students in the 1990s are facing profound, and life-threatening, issues. How to deal with high rates of teenage pregnancy, drug and alcohol abuse and acquired immune deficiency syndrome (AIDS) are unresolved problems of vital concern.

Even after his long absence, Rip Van Winkle would not be unaware of school discipline problems. Bullies were always a presence in the school, intimidating both peers and teachers. But during Rip's 50-year nap, discipline problems have escalated: Now the bullies carry guns and knives. He would be shocked that many schools have security guards and that in some urban schools students are searched for weapons upon entering the building. He might not even recognize the electronic weapons detectors that have been installed in some schools.

Ronald Reagan, in a 1984 speech, cited the alarming extent of disciplinary problems in schools. President Reagan noted that 112,000 secondary students were robbed each month, there were 282,000 physical assaults, 2.4 million thefts of personal belongings and 1,000 teachers each month required a doctor's attention for the injuries inflicted upon them by students.

If Rip consulted the statistics, he would discover that the situation in his community's schools is a nationwide problem. A bleak picture of student behavior was also apparent in a report published in the *Digest of Education Statistics* in 1989. The high school class of 1987 reported that 92.2% had used alcohol. Also, 56.6% reported using an illicit drug (20.8% reported using only marijuana). Marijuana was the most popular illicit drug (50.2%), with cocaine a distant second (15.2%).[1]

After surveying his school and its problems, Rip Van Winkle might also want to seek out a few of his former teachers to see if they had changed. He would still recognize the teacher's basic role as the leader in the classroom. But he would see that the profession of teaching has changed substantially. Let's take a closer look at these changes.

Power to the Teacher

Some in society see a good education as one where the teacher's task is to see to it that students' learning is based on a definite curriculum. This curriculum should be adhered to strictly, whether or not the students actually enjoy learning. Others in society believe a good education is one where the teacher sees to it that children learn to "live democratically," to "cooperate" with one another by developing social skills, even if this means underplaying academic studies.

You may recall the discussion of essentialism and progressive education from the previous chapter. In alternating between these two opposing positions, contemporary teachers are faced with what may be called "cognitive dissonance," that is, they hear two messages that are not easily reconciled. One is to teach the basics whether students "like it or not." The other message is that the primary task of the teacher is to help children "adjust" to their surroundings and that this adjustment is "more important" than teaching subjects.

In a survey of public schoolteachers undertaken by the National Center for Education Information, 77% think that "standards of academic achievement should be flexible enough that every child can feel successful," and 83% feel "schools should adjust to the needs, interests and learning styles of individual students rather than expecting them to accommodate to the norms of the school."[2]

Contributing to this dissonance is the confusion that teachers traditionally feel in making a decision about which position to adopt. In nearly all cases, the teacher's ability to make independent educational decisions is diminished by the school principal or superintendent, board of education or legislature. Teachers are rarely allowed to choose their own teaching method. Because they cannot make such choices, teachers do not have the same freedoms that other professionals have.

As the economist John Kenneth Galbraith reminds us, the little red schoolhouse is remembered, not because it provided a good education, but because ". . . it had a paramount position in the lives of those who attended it that no modern school can hope to attain."[3] Similarly, we remember the teacher of that school because she (the teacher was usually female) was an important person in the community. Today, no teacher can be so important because he or she is not a main role model and educator. Videos and television, newspapers and magazines, museums, movies, and plays all have a strong influence.

When considering the roles of the teacher within society and the school, the formation of teachers' unions must be taken into account. At the turn of the century, teachers began to consider the advantages of forming a union. Through unions, teachers hope to gain an increasing voice in educational policy-making, to provide them with better salaries and working conditions and to offer a sense that they have greater control over their own destiny. Drawing upon the example set by unionized laborers in other fields, teachers have gained the right to bargain collectively with boards of education. The process of collective negotiation is now a time-honored practice in labor relations. Labor unions bargain or negotiate with management about wages, hours, working conditions and other matters having to do with the health, safety and welfare of employees.

Teachers first began talking about forming unions during the early part of the 20th century, and by 1917 the American Federation of Teachers (AFT) was formed. The AFT followed a pattern more typical of labor unions and was formally affiliated with the labor union movement. Among its early members was the distinguished American philosopher John Dewey, who supported teachers in their effort to take a more militant posture and assume a more pivotal role in educational matters. But the movement grew slowly and by 1960 the AFT had but 50,000 members. Its rival, the National Education Association (NEA), had more than 700,000. The NEA was initially formed by school superintendents. It viewed itself as a "professional" organization and was more concerned with the educational rather than the material needs of teachers and other school personnel.

Today, the NEA claims a membership of 1.7 million while the AFT claims no more than 750,000. More than 75% of the nation's teachers are members of one of the unions. The overall growth of teacher unions may be attributed mostly to the growth of the public schools. Expanded school bureaucracies made teachers feel more remote than ever from the sources of decision making and joining a union was a way of having a stronger voice within a larger and increasingly complex system.

As teacher unions grew in power, so did the number of work stoppages or strikes. Teacher strikes were initially illegal since it was widely held that public employees had no right to strike. Moreover, what was a strike of teachers directed against? A public schoolteacher could strike against a board of education which, by itself, could not allocate more money for teachers' salaries than the state legislature would grant. Parents often resented the stoppages, feeling that striking teachers were not desirable role models for children. Was it right for teachers to picket a school? To carry signs and intimidate anyone entering a public school building? Was it fair for striking teachers to deny children an education?

Even though their methods were questioned, teacher unions won concessions from boards of education and state legislatures. They also won grudging acceptance and even respect from the community. Teacher strikes are generally no longer illegal, since the right of public employees to strike was acknowledged by the courts.

Initially, the public viewed teacher unions as an obstacle to progress for the schools, but teacher unions today are becoming engines of reform. However, the unions must balance teachers' demands for better pay, improved working conditions, job security and academic freedom with the community's demand that the teachers be held responsible for their teaching.

The Education of Teachers

Improvements in teacher compensation have been paralleled by better teacher preparation and higher certification requirements. While teachers of the early common school were often scarcely more educated than their students, today's teachers are well-educated individuals who adhere to professional standards dictated by the states in which they teach. Still, as the quality of schools is questioned, the academic preparation of teachers is also being debated, as are differences in certification requirements among the states.

During America's early colonial period, both women and men served as teachers. Gradually, women outnumbered men, and at the elementary level the overwhelming majority of teachers were women. During the early decades of the 19th century, teachers were not expected to have any special kind of training. According to conventions of society at that time, teachers were often the unmarried daughters of good character from prominent families. Teaching was considered the only respectable work available to them. In larger communities, teaching jobs often were the "spoils" of political victory at election time—plums handed out by the victorious political party in exchange for support. For men, who usually taught in the secondary school, teaching was a job until something better came along. For women, teaching was a temporary occupation until marriage. Many of these individuals, however, were dedicated and effective teachers.

The growth of the common school was accompanied by concerns about the formal preparation of teachers. One strong voice on this issue was Calvin Stowe of Ohio, a prominent educator and the husband of Harriet Beecher Stowe, author of *Uncle Tom's Cabin* (1851). In 1837, he urged special post–high school training for potential teachers. The institution associated with his name is the "normal school." The word *normal* is derived from the Latin word for model, or rule. In the normal schools, future teachers would be taught the rules for teaching. The normal school was not considered higher education at all. Instead, its aim was to provide a minimum course of study to those who would teach in the common elementary school. As the common schools grew in number, so did the numbers of teachers, who represented a wide variety of academic backgrounds. The normal school would provide a standard level of training for future teachers, who would be somewhat better informed than their students about spelling, grammar, American history and arithmetic. The major emphasis in the normal school was on techniques, or rules, for teaching. These rules were believed to be effective in teaching the three Rs to children.

How best to prepare future teachers has long been debated, and this debate flares up with regularity in each generation. There are some who believe the only preparation needed for teaching is a liberal arts college degree with a solid background in English and American literature and history, social science and perhaps some science and mathematics. According to this view, instruction in teaching methods is a waste of time.

While few would deny the importance of the liberal arts in the education of teachers, much of the debate centers around how much teachers, especially at the elementary school level, should be taught about teaching methods. Moreover, are those methods best taught in a university setting or directly in the school classroom? The need for instruction in methods of teaching, and some apprenticeship in the classroom, is also widely supported. There is, however, no agreement at all as to how much of each of these ingredients is most desirable. There is also disagreement as to whether formal preparation should occur at the undergraduate or graduate levels of a teacher's college education. Normal schools have disappeared in the United States, and teacher education has become the responsibility of the many colleges and universities that offer programs leading to state certification.

Before they can enter the classroom of a public school and draw a paycheck for their teaching services, teachers must be certified by the state where they wish to teach. Certification means the prospective teacher has met the state's requirements. However, C. Emily Feistritzer, in her 1984 report for the National Center for Education Information (NCIE) titled *The Making of a Teacher*, said: "The certification of classroom teachers in the U.S. is a mess. Each state makes its own rules concerning who can be certified and what they can be certified to teach. The numbers of different types of certificates and what is required to get one within a state, much less nationwide, are staggering."[4] Thus, a person certified to teach math in Illinois may not be able to do so in Alabama. A teacher certified to teach American history in California may not be able to do so in New York without taking additional courses.

Teacher Satisfaction

Are teachers happy with their chosen profession? According to NCIE research reported in 1990, of the 2.4 million teachers in this nation's public schools (approximately 71% of them women) about one-fourth said they were unhappy with their situation, feeling underpaid and unappreciated for their work. Regarding pay, teachers are less and less satisfied with their standard of living.[5]

Although teachers' salaries have risen 77% since 1980–81, this does not include an adjustment for inflation (higher prices). When inflation is taken into account, the true rise in salaries has been only about 20%.[6]

Regarding the need for society to appreciate the important role that educators play in the development of children, the respect that teachers deserve still lags behind other professions. While a businesswoman may acknowledge—and pay handsomely for—her lawyer's presentation on her behalf, that same businesswoman is less prone to appreciate—and compensate— the teacher's contribution to her child's education and development. Parents, children and society at large need to give greater recognition to the crucial role that teachers play.[7]

Are There Enough Teachers?

Balancing the supply of teachers with the number of children entering the schools at any one time means there are periods of a few years when there are too many teachers, and other times when there are not enough.

In some areas, particularly math and science, teachers are known to be in short supply. Part of the reason for this shortage is that although teaching was the first choice among many women years ago, it is now weighed against many competing career options in business and government. Women now have opportunities in a wide variety of other fields where they can gain respect, prestige and higher incomes.

Moreover, there are some who believe the bureaucratic jungle that state certification has created also serves to discourage a considerable number of the 34 million adult Americans who have at least one college degree and may want to become teachers. This is especially true for those capable men and women who are considering changes in career, say from business or other professions into teaching. And many able scholars, who do not have the range of courses required for state certification, are barred from teaching.

In an attempt to remedy this situation and to attract able people to the teaching profession, many states have developed alternate routes to state certification. These alternatives are designed to make it possible for men and women to make mid-career changes into education, if they have at least an undergraduate college degree. While they teach, they must, however, complete the necessary academic and methods courses, generally after school hours or during summers.

Alternate routes to teaching also help communities to recruit college-educated men and women of varied racial and ethnic backgrounds. This helps urban schools to achieve a teaching staff in harmony with the racial mix of students. "At least one-third of the nation's school children will be members of minorities by the end of this decade, but only about 10 percent of the nation's teachers are black, Asian or Hispanic. The number of aspiring teachers who are members of minorities is even smaller, about 8 percent."[8] As a greater number of minority men and women become teachers, they will serve as positive role models to their students, encouraging minority children to see the classroom as a place where they, too, can have a career.

Should Television Teach?

Almost 30 years ago, Professor Thomas Clark Pollock of New York University declared, "It now seems clear that television offers the greatest opportunity for the advancement of education since the introduction of movable type."[9] While television has helped alter the American character and change our values and life-styles, television has scarcely made a dent in the way children are formally educated. While its influence, for better or worse, is universal, the high hopes of the past for experimenting with television as a teaching device have yet to bear fruit. It is clear that television has the power to command our attention. Nearly everyone—about 98% of American families—has a TV set. But can television teach?

The answer to this question is an emphatic "yes." Television teaches us which soap to buy, which toothpaste to use, which deodorant will get us our next job. Public television programs offer another dimension of entertainment. Programs about art, history, physics, government or almost anything else can focus on a detail of an experiment or a technique of drawing, and can bring what is being discussed so close to the eyes of the viewer that he or she is closer to what is happening than in an actual classroom.

Television was once thought of as appropriate only to large group instruction. And for this purpose it is clearly useful, but today's television need not only be used for instructing large groups. Videotapes allow a single viewer to watch any program and rerun it until what is being taught is mastered. Programs modeled after "Sesame Street," for instance, can teach the alphabet and basics of reading to children. For foreign language instruction, there is little better than video instruction for drill and practice.

There are difficulties, however, in adapting television effectively to the schools. Getting good and clear television reception is not always easy in many schools; sophisticated and expensive cable equipment and comfortable facilities are often in short supply.

Television is also resisted by teachers who assert that television intrudes on their lesson plans and distracts them from traditional teaching methods. Making use of television can disrupt the lesson plan and require completely different approaches to managing the classroom because it is often not taken seriously by students. Teachers fear that students associate television with relaxation and leisure and assume that, when sitting in front of a television set, they will be entertained or amused rather than taught.

Film and video can miseducate as easily as they educate. But these media are everywhere and are a force that schools can enlist in their quest for improvement. As new technology makes available hundreds of new channels of televised instruction, it will become easier to tailor programs to the needs of individuals and small groups. Television will not go away. Given the technology that is emerging, learning by television and video instruction outside the school is at least a technological possibility. Should interactive television become widespread, allowing viewers to respond to the TV teachers' questions and instruction, it is possible for learning through this medium to at least supplement the classroom.

Computers represent another modern teaching method. Although they are widely available in most schools, however, computers have not become central to the way education is "delivered." While the world is being shaken by a revolution in telecommunications, with computer and video technology both at the heart of it, schools do not yet appear to be tangibly affected.

Beyond the obvious problems of adequate supplies of devices such as televisions, VCRs and computers is a more fundamental issue. The basic structure and organization of schools and teaching methods are not very different from what they were 50 years ago. This may have to change. The new technology may have to be imposed on classrooms; teachers can be urged to use television and computers to complement their teaching. The use of the computer, for example, needs to be integrated into the teaching plan so that students spend part of each day interacting with the computer, being led through problem-solving exercises that expand on the information being discussed in class. Technology does not replace teachers but helps them to be more effective.

The restructuring of schools has to come first, so that the technology is used in harmony with other, more traditional methods of instruction. New technologies alone have not been initiators of change in the classroom.

Education and the Invisible Hand

In his book on what makes the economy work, *The Wealth of Nations* (1776), the economist Adam Smith held that every person, even in making selfish choices, is "led by an *invisible hand* to promote an end which was no part of his intention. By pursuing his own interest he frequently promotes that of society more effectually than when he really intends to promote it." Adam Smith is saying that in the long run, the choices we make among competing goods and services not only help the individual but guide society's development as well.

Critics of the current state of America's schools suggest that by offering parents a choice of schools for their children to attend, the overall quality of education would improve. They claim that, basically, less effective schools would not be patronized and would close, while more effective ones would attract an ever increasing number of pupils. Thus, in the act of choosing, parents and students would also be led by an *invisible hand*. In the process of selecting good schools over poor ones, the good schools would flourish, the bad ones would close, and society as a whole would be served because only good schools would survive. Let's take a closer look at what this philosophy means for education.

Since the development of the common school, initiated over 150 years ago, the notion of choice in education is probably the most revolutionary reform to be proposed as a solution to the problems of America's schools. In our current system of education, each state has a monopoly on public schools and even substantial control over nonpublic ones. Moreover, in each school district, children are usually assigned to public schools by school authorities, mostly on the basis of where their families live. As a result, most children at most times could not choose the schools they preferred to attend, assuming they do not prefer the ones closest to home. And yet, there is a loophole in this system; that is, parents who are concerned about the schools their children attend can move to school districts they believe offer a better education. Affluent parents who are willing and able to pay higher taxes can actively choose better-funded schools by choosing to reside in other school districts. Often this means moving from the inner city to the suburbs, from districts where schools tend to be large and impersonal to those where they tend to be smaller and offer more personalized opportunities and services (though these schools are not necessarily better in terms of the education that students receive).

In a report titled *Time for Results*, issued in 1986, a task force of state governors had the following to say about making choice possible:

Presently, the school system controls both the production and consumption of education. The system tells the students what they will learn, at what speed, and what quality. Students and their parents have little to say about it. A more responsive system would incorporate what students and their parents say they need with the education services necessary to meet it.[10]

But does choice open more questions and create more problems than it solves? Does allowing parents and children to choose undermine the public school system? Does choice destroy whatever racial and ethnic diversity has been achieved in public education? Should students and their parents have the opportunity to choose nonpublic schools as well? If the school has a religious affiliation, is this a violation of separation of church and state as provided in the First Amendment of the U.S. Constitution? Do parents and students really have sufficient knowledge to choose? Do they really know what a good school is? Let's take a closer look at several of these complicated questions.

Educators believe the single most important reform needed in public education is the involvement of parents. Because of the critical nature of parental involvement, eight states, led by Minnesota in 1985, have adopted plans to allow parents to register their children in any public schools in the state, based on a "voucher" that is based on the amount of state funding allocated for each child's education. It is hoped that by allowing parents and children to choose, parents will be encouraged to monitor their children's performance and take a greater interest in the activities of the school.

Most public school administrators and teachers oppose choice plans because they fear they will undermine the public school system, reintroduce segregation and, in general, discriminate against the poor. It is feared that only the more sophisticated and affluent parents will take full advantage of choice, particularly in a system that requires a financial contribution from the parents. Educators are also concerned that poor and disadvantaged children won't gain because their families may not have the resources or knowledge to help them benefit from the new options. With the exodus of affluent children (who are likely not to be members of minority groups), the progress made thus far in integrating the public schools would also be diminished.

Those who favor choice, however, insist that competition among schools will improve education. They claim that this is an example of market economy applied to education: Those schools that are underenrolled because they were not chosen will deservedly fade away.

In Milwaukee in 1989, Wisconsin State Representative Polly Williams asserted that forced busing of children to achieve integration was failing to improve the education of children. She proposed, instead, a choice plan allowing 1,000 children from families with very low incomes to attend private nonsectarian schools. Although some schools would not be racially integrated, she claimed that through parental choice children would be better educated. Schools chosen by the children's parents would be given a voucher good for up to $2,500 in state funds. All the teachers and administrators and their associations opposed the choice plan. The NAACP likewise opposed the idea with the opinion that greater segregation in the public schools would be the unfortunate result.

When the circuit court upheld the Milwaukee school choice plan, the city's school superintendent, Herbert J. Grover, declared in opposition to the court's decision, "We will have everyone fleeing the public school."[11] Others in the black community, however, led by Representative Polly Williams, hailed the decision as an effective alternative to a "bankrupt" public school system.

This victory was short-lived, as the Wisconsin State Court of Appeals ruled the plan unconstitutional. Since this ruling was based on a technicality rather than on the actual content of the proposal, further appeals are sure to be made. The Milwaukee choice plan is more radical than most since it incorporates a limited number of nonpublic, nonsectarian schools into its program as well as public schools.

In their book, *Politics, Markets, and America's Schools* (1990), John E. Chubb and Terry M. Moe, political science researchers at the Brookings Institution, a research organization in Washington, D.C., advocate a broadly gauged plan of school choice. In their plan, any organization that wishes to create a school may do so if it meets minimum state certification criteria. Existing public and private schools would also be required to apply for such certification. Every pupil would be free to attend any school in the state. Each school would then be eligible to receive a fee from the state based on the number of pupils enrolled. Free transportation would be provided to make choice a reality for those who may select schools located at any great distance from their homes.

Each school would be free to establish its own admissions standards, provided such standards do not discriminate on the basis of race. State certification requirements for teachers would remain a responsibility of the state, but Chubb and Moe urge they be kept minimal. Sectarian schools would not be able to participate because of the controversy regarding public funds going to religiously affiliated schools. Chubb and Moe hope this obstacle could be overcome.[12]

There are many proposals for choice in education and no clear pattern has yet emerged; some proposals are concerned with choice among public schools; others include public and private, nonsectarian schools. Still others seek to broaden freedom of choice to include parochial, or religious, schools. Regardless of the specific provisions in the plans, however, they are designed to provide parents with a greater array of options, while giving schools more freedom from regulation over the programs they offer, the teachers they hire and the students they serve. Those who support greater choice in education also believe the community will be held more accountable for the quality of its schools because parents could "vote with their feet," by choosing to send or to withdraw their children from a particular school and make their tax-provided dollars available elsewhere. Supporters also believe competition for students will be an incentive for teachers to sharpen their teaching skills, and make school administrators more eager to serve students' special needs, including those of the disabled.

In April 1991, when President George Bush formally presented his educational reform initiative, America 2000, he also stated his support of school funding plans similar to the Milwaukee proposal, with parents given the amount of state aid allocated for their children's education as a voucher spent as desired at a public or a private school. This plan would create an educational "market," with parents and students in the role of consumer. It is predicted by the plan's supporters that with this freedom, some less affluent students could attend private schools, private schools would have needed financial support and public schools would have the incentive to improve. Still, educators have valid concerns that such programs could lead to the neglect of the public schools, slow down school integration and penalize the poor.

Some people compare the voucher plan to Adam Smith's economic theory, with the education "market" operating in parallel with Smith's concept of the free market: In seeking their own interests, parents and students would also be led by an invisible hand that promotes the interests of society. The good schools would thrive and society would be further enriched. But what is a good school?

A Good School

If parents are free to choose a school for their child, how will they recognize a good one? Fortunately, it may be easier to recognize a good school when one actually sees and experiences one than it is to define one.

Of two schools with essentially similar resources, one may be better than the other, even by a wide margin. Why? In 1979, Michael Rutter and his associates in England began a study to investigate why this could be so. They studied 12 secondary schools in working-class sections of London and discovered, as did Coleman, that tangible resources do not necessarily contribute to or explain differences in the achievement of pupils. What does?

According to the Rutter report, the following factors do correlate with pupil achievement:

1. A good school, that is, one that obtains high levels of student achievement, is one in which learning is deemed important.
2. A good school is one where there is good discipline.
3. A good school is one where teachers plan their lessons carefully, are generous in praise and assign homework regularly.[13]

Rutter described these factors as the "ethos" or prevailing atmosphere of the school. That is, the good school is one that fosters high morale and school spirit, not merely for the conquests of the athletic teams, but in recognizing academic achievement and pursuits. A school that demands and expects much from its students, but also helps them to achieve more, is the kind of school parents would choose for their children.

The problem with these criteria is that while good schools can be recognized, there is little agreement on how they can best be created. If an experiment in a scientific laboratory can be repeated thousands of times with the same results, there is considerable confidence it will always work that way. In education, however, the results of experiments are difficult to repeat. What may be successful for one small group of children may not be successful with another small group, and may be entirely ineffective in a large one. What may work in one geographical area may not work at all in another.

The leadership of the principal is important in establishing an environment that is conducive to learning, but a principal who is successful at one school may be ineffective at another. Hard-working teachers, a mix of students based on ability as well as on race, effective discipline, the diligent assignment and performance of homework—these factors might combine to make a highly effective school. However, it is difficult to know in advance which kinds of resources, such as additional teachers and supplies, will be needed to achieve the desired results. What makes a good school is a special mix of human beings— teachers, administrators and students—and humans cannot be predicted and controlled like chemicals in a laboratory. Because of these circumstances, educational leaders need to make a wide variety of learning styles available to parents and pupils so they may choose what works best for them.

Niche marketing, now emerging in industry, may be relevant in the future of education. The technique holds that through technological advances it is possible to reach smaller groups, or niches, of people in an economical manner. For example, computers store mailing lists that can be sorted so advertisements are only sent to people with certain interests and characteristics. In parallel fashion, it should be possible to provide cost-effective "niche" education to groups of children with similar but relatively narrow learning interests (e.g., science, music, performing arts, politics). Niche education seems the opposite of the common school, with all students sitting side by side, regardless of their differences in background and aptitude, and receiving an "equal" education. However, niche education also provides a means of reaching all students in the diverse environment of today's schools. By giving each school a sense of mission, perhaps even of destiny, an environment that supports learning may be encouraged.

In short, the education of the masses need no longer be provided on a mass basis and enforced by a huge bureaucracy.

Just as the "invisible hand" works effectively in the market-place, so, too, the "invisible hand" of parental and student choice may make good schools the universal rule.

In summary, alternative routes to teacher certification have been proposed as a means of improving teaching and rebuilding the profession. Choice of schools is proposed as a means of more effectively enlisting the parents' participation in the schools their children attend. The more widespread application of technology to instruction may offer a high-tech response to the educational needs of the next century. But if one were to formulate an educational agenda for the next century, what would it look like?

Suggestions for change are outlined in Chapter Seven.

Notes

Citations in the notes are brief. Full citations appear in the bibliography.

CHAPTER SIX

1. Snyder, 134–35.
2. Feistritzer, *The Wall Street Journal*, October 26, 1990.
3. Galbraith, 257.
4. Feistritzer. *The Making of a Teacher*, 361.
5. Feistritzer, *The Wall Street Journal*, October 26, 1990.
6. Ibid.
7. Ibid.
8. *The New York Times*, August 28, 1990.
9. Lewis, 41.
10. Lamm, 12.
11. *The New York Times*, August 8, 1990.
12. Wilson, 39.
13. Ibid

An Agenda for the Twenty-first Century

Throughout the pages of this book, the hopes, the shortcomings, the successes, the challenges and the multitude of issues facing America's public schools have been chronicled and examined, starting with the earliest days of the common school. Because of the complexities of our society, and the many responsibilities the schools must juggle, we've seen that inevitably the schools cannot always meet our demands.

We will conclude our look at the public schools with examples of forces at work in the world outside the classroom, the neighborhoods, parents' groups, state and federal legislatures and their impact on what happens inside the classroom. It's important to consider these forces before passing judgment on our educational system. From there, suggestions for reforms, including America 2000, will be discussed.

The Real World of the Schools

Because public schools function under the control of the communities they serve, children's education reflects this public environment as well as the broader concerns and issues embroiling American society. Students spend a few limited

123

hours a day in school. What happens to them—and what they are exposed to—during the non-school hours cannot be left out on the steps when they enter the school building. This has always been true.

The following are some vivid and poignant examples of how public education reflects the current social and political landscape.

- Among the children at School 36 in Rochester, New York, is a fifth-grade girl who has changed schools eight times since kindergarten. She is one of nine children and has been shuttled between her father and stepmother, her grandmother and her mother for as long as she can remember. With each move has come a transfer to a new school. Of her first two, she says, "I don't remember nobody there."[1] How can schools best provide for children who change schools so frequently? What is the obligation of the schools? Of other agencies?

- A fifth-grader in New York City's P.S. 57 is a young school dropout who stays at home watching cartoons or pedaling his bicycle past decayed, graffiti-covered buildings, on streets littered with the evidence of drug abuse. To help youngsters like him, an increasing number of social workers are attempting to intervene at an earlier age by making sure a child has food and clothing and by offering family advice to try to make it possible for them to stay in school longer.[2] Will such intercession work? Can a critical mass of potential dropouts be reached effectively?

- The children in a school in East Harlem in New York City cannot look out of their classroom windows. The teacher has them working on a project to paste white stars against a black background that represents the sky. The entire sheet will be placed over the glass windows so the children will not see drug addicts shooting up in their school yard.[3]

Can public schools stand up against the problems of the community without being brought down?

- At P.S. 192 in New York City's Harlem, teachers and their principal are conferring on important policies and practices and reaching decisions once made only by the principal. "Power sharing," as this is called, is an initiative of city school chancellor Joseph A. Fernandez, who came to the New York schools in 1990. It is hoped that when teachers and administrators together decide what is best for the children in their school, students will receive a better education and teachers will have higher morale.[4] However, power sharing is new to both teachers and school administrators, and both are raising the question, "Will it work?" Approaching the process cautiously, both groups are giving it a try.

- In 1988, the average public school teacher of the wealthy Boston suburb of Belmont, Massachusetts, earned $36,100. Only 3% of the community's 18-year-olds dropped out of high school. More than 89% of its graduating seniors planned to attend four-year colleges. In the nearby community of Chelsea, the average public school teacher in 1988 earned $26,200; more than half of the community's 18-year-olds dropped out. Only 10% planned to go on to college.[5] How can such disparities in community support for teachers and schools be overcome?

- Educational disparity is often glaring when considering the amount of taxpayer money spent per student from community to community and state to state. Consider Highland Park High School in an affluent suburb of Dallas, Texas. The students of Highland Park have use of a planetarium, indoor swimming pool, closed-circuit TV studio and first-class science laboratory. The community spends about $6,000 to educate each student. According to Texas education officials, the richest school district in the state spends $19,300 per pupil; the poorest, $2,100.[6] Not only is this an example of great differences in educational opportunity, but it becomes a local map of social class and ethnic diversity. The rich school districts are largely white while poor ones consist mainly of racial minorities. Is the segregation caused by racial discrimination or economic differences? If *de facto* segregation results from economic differences, what can be done about it?

In spite of the odds, schools are also rising to the challenge through innovative programs that make learning an exciting experience for students.

- Children become teenagers during the middle school years, and this can be a difficult time. The Henry Eggers Middle School in Hammond, Indiana, has instituted small learning communities with students taught by the same team of teachers for three years. They become an extended family during this time, helping to ease the preteen to teenage transition. The school has also instituted a program called the "three Cs"—coping, caring, and communicating—to address issues such as drug and alcohol abuse, suicide and teenage pregnancy.[7]
- In multicultural neighborhoods, students often come from homes where the parents do not speak English and may be poorly educated as well. Through the PTA (Parent-Teacher Association), the John James Audubon Elementary School in San Diego, California, has enlisted the cooperation of parents in encouraging their children to learn. Spanish-speaking parents volunteer in their children's classrooms and learn English and other skills along with their children. The school

has also instituted reading programs that encourage parental involvement.[8]

The common school was born in the belief that public schools can educate *all* our nation's children and remain academically demanding as well. Achieving educational equity, or fairness, for all means not only helping average and poor students learn but also challenging the more able students creatively and intellectually. How can schools maintain equity and excellence—serve and meet the needs of *all* students? This has been the charge and the dilemma of the common school from the very beginning. If the common school has strayed from the plan originally laid out for it, the following suggestions may help set it back on course.

Toward Better Schools

In 1991, 45 million children attend primary and secondary public schools in the United States. This is about the same number as did a decade ago. Even when inflation is taken into account, $79 billion more was spent on education in 1990 than in 1980.[9] Since substantially more money is being spent to educate the same number of students in our schools as 10 years ago, it is clear that simply spending more is not the answer to making schools better. We need to be smarter about how we spend.

A Longer School Year

In 1983, *A Nation at Risk* urged a longer school year. It recommended adopting a seven-hour school day and a 200- to 220-day school year.[10] A longer school day is needed so in-depth study can be encouraged on a host of complex issues and subjects. During a longer day, individualized remedial instruction can be provided and the able student inspired.

A longer school year would more closely match that of other industrialized countries. To the extent that our economy is linked to an educated people, a longer school year would make the nation more competitive by allowing more time for learning.

In 1985, the distinguished economist Lester Thurow of the Massachusetts Institute of Technology strongly endorsed the proposal for a longer academic year. He declared a preference for a shorter school year was a form of American arrogance. He wrote: "Americans think they can learn in 180 days what the rest of the world takes 220 to 240 days to learn. It also forgets that the rest of the world is trying to use its 220 to 240 days more efficiently."[11]

Early Education

It is essential that schooling begin for children at about age three. Studies from Head Start and other programs demonstrate that children can develop mentally, emotionally and physically from early and systematic intervention in the learning process. The studies demonstrating the success of Head Start have already been noted as has the decision by Congress to extend Head Start to all eligible children. (See page 69.)

Programs for the Gifted

The brightest children remain our most neglected resource. The National Commission on Excellence in Education commented: "Today, gifted and talented students are often overlooked. Teachers and administrators just assume they'll 'make it,' and 'blossom on their own.' Nothing could be farther from the truth."[12] *A Nation at Risk* noted that ". . . the ideal of academic excellence as the primary goal of schooling seems to be fading across the board in American education."[13]

The best and the brightest among our youth are not pushed hard enough to learn. Compared with gifted youth in other countries, for example, they take less math and less science. According to the International Association for the Evaluation of Educational Achievement (IEA), in a 1981–82 study, a very small percentage of American 12th graders studied advanced mathematics. Fifty percent of Hungarian students studied advanced math, as did 30% of the students in British Columbia and 15% of Finnish students. Only 13% of students in the United States studied advanced math.[14] Yet, these young adults will be at the cutting edge of whatever tomorrow brings. Their intellectual development needs to be made a matter of high national priority. The British philosopher Alfred North Whitehead, in his book, *The Aims of Education*, noted, "The nation that does not value trained intelligence is doomed."

Smaller Schools
Small schools appear to be preferable to large ones. Indeed, one of the strong arguments for allowing parents to choose schools for their children is that the selection of a small school would be made possible. In district four in East Harlem in New York City in the early 1980s, the superintendent set up 44 small schools in his attempt to improve reading scores. Smaller school size helped move the district from the poorest reading scores to about the middle of the range.[15]

Use of Educational Technology
The revolution in technology and communications, including cable TV, video and computers, can make schools more efficient and responsive to children's needs. Schools need to follow developments in these fields and adapt their school facilities and schedules to use them most effectively. Even though it is often thought of as contributing to a dehumaniz-

ing and impersonal society, technology also has within it the possibility to be cost effective in providing individual as well as group instruction.

Corporate Involvement

Many large businesses and educational institutions are participating in collaborative ventures. These have not yet made an overall impact on education. Businesspeople and educators need to get together to determine job standards— at least for entry-level jobs—and then hold them open for students who stay in school and prepare themselves. Moreover, some activities that schools currently undertake can be "privatized," that is, performed by private industry. Driver education is an important example. Schools and industry should make some decisions about how they can work together to help our students choose careers and enter the working world.

College and University Involvement

Many colleges and universities have formed collaborative ventures with elementary and secondary schools. The most interesting experiment in school/college collaboration today is the Boston University School of Education's attempt to administer the schools of Chelsea, Massachusetts. Chelsea's schools, mentioned earlier in this chapter, have a high dropout rate. Though it is much too early to say how this effort will turn out, is it an act of educational statesmanship or mere arrogance on the part of the university to think it can do better? Yale has done significant work with the schools of New Haven, Connecticut, and has met with some success.

Yet, despite success, university and school collaborations have not yet demonstrated the impact they *can* have. School and college schedules need to coincide more effectively. College professors need to be given more credit toward tenure and promotion for working collaboratively with the schools. For public schools and public colleges, some form of budget sharing would help solve the problem of who pays for what when the institutions to cooperate on a project.

Community Involvement

Able and creative men and women from the professional community should be brought into the school for short and even irregular intervals. The creative use of a host of talented people can provide alternative instructional activities, role models for children, as well as stimulating and interesting opportunities for interaction with educators. Alternative routes to teacher certification (see page 111) may make this happen.

Community Service Internships

Teenagers should be encouraged to perform some kind of community service as part of their requirements for high school graduation. This idea has been explored by the Carnegie Foundation for the Advancement of Teaching. Ernest L. Boyer, its president, reports his interview with a high school junior who finds that even work at McDonalds, which she describes as unexciting, makes her ". . . feel that I'm an adult person, that I'm doing something useful. In school, you never feel that way. Not ever."[16] The Carnegie Foundation report goes on to urge that ". . . young people should be given opportunities to reach beyond themselves and feel more responsively engaged. They should be encouraged to participate in the communities of which they are a part. Therefore, we recommend that every high school student complete a service requirement . . . involving volunteer work in the community or at school."[17] A further extension of this is a proposal endorsed by William Buckley, publisher of the *National Review*, and others, for a system of national service requiring all young men and women to spend a year after high school working full-time for a voluntary organization.

An Educational Agenda for the Twenty-first Century

With his America 2000 educational proposal, President Bush drew the nation's attention to the concerns of educators, and that is in itself a valuable service. Hopefully, it will lead to new initiatives needed for the current generation of students now in our schools, as well as those in the near future. These groups will be doing their most productive work during the first quarter of the next century.

However, action is the key to constructive change in the schools, as it has always been. James Boswell, the biographer of Samuel Johnson, England's distinguished 18th-century literary scholar, reported Johnson's views on the subject of education. In a discussion of what should be taught first in school, Johnson had this to say: "Sir, there is no matter what you teach them first, any more than what leg you shall put into your breeches [trousers] first. Sir, you may stand disputing which is best to put in first, but in the meantime your backside is bare." As the 20th century draws to a close, we are again debating how best to educate the nation's youth in the formal setting of the schools. However, while the debate goes on, the schools mark time.

The common school was created to provide not only intellectual and vocational preparation but also to ensure the survival of democracy and the American way of life. Our progress as a democracy in the 21st century depends on how well we nurture and develop our schools, to guarantee the best possible opportunity for learning to all Americans.

Take a close look at what's going on around you in your school—the energy of students and teachers, the new knowledge and skills acquired, and the events and activities that help round out the whole experience of education. This is the essence of the schools' contribution to society, just as it has been since the earliest common school. Of course, because human beings are not perfect, neither are schools. Yet, it is the natural human urge for self-improvement that enables the school system to grow, change and thrive.

What are the best aspects of your school? What could be improved? Think about this as you complete your education and go on to become a voting member of your community. Your ideas and actions will help determine the future.

Notes

Citations in the notes are brief. Full citations appear in the bibliography.

CHAPTER SEVEN

1. *The Wall Street Journal*, November 14, 1990.
2. *The New York Times*, November 14, 1990.
3. *The New York Daily News*, October 19, 1990.
4. *The New York Times*, November 13, 1990.
5. Reich, 44.
6. Ibid., 45.
7. *Newsweek*, March 12, 1990.
8. Ibid.
9. National Commission on Excellence in Education, 29.
10. Barrett, 100.
11. Boyer, 202.
12. National Commission on Excellence in Education, 14.
13. Barrett, 85–86.
14. Leo, 17.
15. Boyer, 202.
16. Ibid., 209.
17. Ibid.

Bibliography

Adler, Mortimer. *The Padeia Proposal.* New York: Macmillan, 1982.

Ayers, Leonard P. *Laggards in Our Schools: A Study of Retardation and Elimination in City School Systems.* New York: Russell Sage Foundation, 1909.

Barrett, Michael J. "The Case for More School Days." *The Atlantic Monthly* 266 (November, 1990).

Bernstein, Richard. "A War of Words." *New York Times Magazine* (October 14, 1990).

Bestor, Arthur. *Educational Wastelands.* Urbana, Ill.: University of Illinois Press, 1953.

Boyer, Ernest L. *High School: A Report on Secondary Education in America.* New York: Harper and Row, 1983.

Braddock II, Jomills, Henry, et al. "A Long-Term View of School Desegregation: Some Recent Studies of Graduates as Adults." *Phi Delta Kappan,* 66 (December 1984).

Brameld, Theodore. *Patterns of Educational Philosophy.* New York: World Book Company, 1950.

Butts, R. Freeman and Cremin, Lawrence A. *A History of Education in American Culture.* New York: Holt, Rinehart and Winston, 1953.

Covello, Leonard. *The Heart is the Teacher.* New York: McGraw-Hill, 1958.

Copperman, Paul. *The Literary Hoax: the Decline of Reading, Writing, and Learning in the Public Schools and What We Can Do About It.* New York: William Morrow, 1978.

Cremin, Lawrence. *The Genius of American Education.* New York: Vintage Books, 1966.

———. *Public Education.* New York: Basic Books, 1976.

D'Aimee, Lys. "The Menace of Present Educational Methods," *Gunton's Magazine* 19 (September 1900).

Dewey, John. *The School and Society* [A series of lectures, edited by Jo Ann Boydston]. Carbondale, Ill.: Southern Illinois University Press, 1980.

Education Commission of the States. *Action for Excellence: A Comprehensive Plan to Improve Our Nation's Schools.* Washington, D.C., 1983.

Feistritzer, C. Emily. *The Making of a Teacher.* Washington, D.C.: The

National Center for Education Information, 1984.

———. "Not Happy Teachers—Better Teachers." *Wall Street Journal* (October 26, 1990).

Galbraith, John Kenneth. *The Affluent Society.* Boston: Houghton, Mifflin Co., 1958.

Goodlad, John. *A Place Called School.* New York: McGraw-Hill, 1984.

Graham, Ellen. "Lost in the Shuffle: In Inner City Schools, Endless Transfers Hurt Some Students' Work," *Wall Street Journal* (November 14, 1990).

Greer, Colin. *The Great School Legend.* New York: Basic Books, Inc., 1972.

Honeywell, Roy J. *The Educational Work of Thomas Jefferson.* "Report of the Commissioners Appointed to Fix the Site of the University of Virginia." Cambridge, MA: Harvard University Press, 1931.

Horne, Herman H. *A Democratic Philosophy of Education.* New York: Macmillan, 1932.

Hutchins, Robert. *The Conflict in Education in a Democratic Society.* New York: Harper and Brothers, 1953.

International Association for the Evaluation of Educational Achievement. *Fortune Magazine* (Spring 1990).

Kirsch, Irwin S. and Jungeblut, Ann. *Literacy: Profiles in America's Young Adults.* National Assessment of Educational Progress, Report 16-PL-02. Princeton, NJ: Educational Testing Service, 1986.

Kozol, Jonathan. "Children at Risk," *Newsweek* (March 12, 1990).

Lamm, Richard D. "Task Force on Parent Involvement and Choice." *National Governors' Association.* Washington, D.C., 1986.

Leo, John. "School Reforms Best Choice." *U. S. News and World Report* (January 14, 1991).

Lewis, Philip. *Educational Television: A Guidebook.* New York: McGraw-Hill, 1961.

Mann, Horace. *Lectures and Annual Reports on Education.* Cambridge, MA: The Editor, 1867.

Marriott, Michel. "Dropout Fight Is Retooled for Grade Schools," *New York Times* (November 14, 1990).

Myrdal, Gunnar. *An American Dilemma.* New York: Harper and Brothers, 1944.

National Center for Children in Poverty, School of Public Health, Columbia University. "Five Million Children: A Statistical Profile of our Poorest Young Citizens." New York: Columbia University Press, 1990.

National Commission on Excellence in Education. *A Nation at Risk: The Imperative for Educational Reform.* Washington, D.C.: Government Printing Office, 1983.

National Science Board Commission on Pre-College Education in Mathematics, Science and Technology. *Educating Americans for the 21st Century.* Washington, D.C.: 1983.

The New York Times. Feb. 10, 1970; Aug. 8, 1990; Aug. 28, 1990; Nov. 14, 1990; Nov. 13, 1991.

Ravitch, Diane. "Schools Without Bureaucracy—Here in N.Y.C.," *New York Daily News* (October 19, 1990).

————. The Troubled Crusade. New York: Basic Books, Inc., 1983.

Rice, Joseph Mayer. *The Public School System of the United States.* New York: The Century Company, 1893.

Sadler, Michael E. "Impressions of American Education," *Educational Review* 25 (March, 1903).

Schultz, Theodore W. *The Economic Value of Education.* New York: Columbia University Press, 1963.

Silberman, Charles. "A Devastating Report on U.S. Education." *Fortune Magazine* (August 1967).

————. *Crisis in the Classroom.* New York: Vintage Books, 1971.

Snyder, Thomas D. *Digest of Education Statistics.* Washington, D.C.: U.S. Government Printing Office, 1989.

Tocqueville, Alexis de. *Democracy in America.* New York: Vintage Books, 1961.

Twentieth-Century Fund Task Force on Federal Elementary and Secondary Education Policy. *Making The Grade.* New York: Twentieth-Century Fund, 1983.

U.S. Congress, House Subcommittee on Elementary, Secondary, and Vocational Education of the Committee on Education and Labor, *Bilingual Education*, 95th Congress, 1st Session, 1977.

Wilson, James Q. "Multiple Choice Test." *The New Republic* (October 8, 1990).

Wolfthal, Maurice. "The Way We Were: Students in the Golden Age." *Daedalus* 113, 1984.

INDEX

Academy, 18
Acquired immune deficiency syndrome (AIDS), 103
Action for Excellence: A Comprehensive Plan to Improve Our Nation's Schools (1983), 11
Adams, John, 36
Adler, Mortimer, 77–78
AIDS—*See Acquired immune deficiency syndrome*
Aims of Education, The, 129
Alcohol abuse, 97–98, 103, 104
Alger, Horatio, 39
Alliance for Better Chicago Schools, 101
Alternate certification, 111, 131
American Dilemma, An, 58
American English, 43–44
American Federation of Labor (AFL), 41
American Federation of Teachers (AFT), 1, 106
American history, 42–43
Americanization: bilingual education and, 67–69; schools and, 37
American Missionary Society, 53
American Revolution, 36
America 2000, 1, 12–13, 119, 132
Aristotle, 77

Back-to-basics movement, 87–90
Bagley, William C., 80
Barnard, Henry, 27
Basic skills: common school, 21; essentialism, 79; normal school, 108; progressivism, 84
Bell, Terrell, 9, 68
Belmont (Massachusetts), 125
Bennett, William J., 68–69
Bestor, Arthur, 86–89
Bilingual education, 66–69
Bilingual Education Act (1968), 67
Bill for the More General Diffusion of Knowledge (Virginia, 1779), 19
Bill of Rights (Amendments 1-10), 24
Biology, teaching of, 92–93
Black Codes, 54
Blacks: common school, 22; late 19th century South, 54–56; Re-

construction South, 53–54; "separate but equal" policy, 23; World War II and after, 56–66
Blue-Backed Speller, 37
Board of Education v. Allen (1962), 95
Boards of education: teacher strikes and, 107
Boston University, 130
Boswell, James, 132
Boyer, Ernest L., 11, 131
British Columbia, 129
Brookings Institution, 118
Brown v. the Board of Education of Topeka, Kansas (1954), 23, 58–60, 65
Bryan, William Jennings, 91
Buckley, William, 131–132
Buildings, public school, 102
Bush, George, 1, 12–13, 119, 132
Business, role of, 38
Busing, 64–65, 95

"Cafeteria" style curriculum, 10
Capitalism, 117
Carnegie Foundation for the Advancement of Teaching, 131
Catcher in the Rye, 103
Centennial Exhibition (Philadelphia, 1876), 40
Central High School (Little Rock, Arkansas), 58–59
Certification, 109–111, 118
Chelsea (Massachusetts), 130
Chicago, 101
Child-centered education, 30–31
Child labor laws, 48
Choice of schools, 114–119
Christmas, Florence, 57
Chubb, John E., 117–118
Civic virtue, 44
Civil Rights, U.S. Commission on, 64
Civil Rights Act (1875), 55
Civil Rights Act (1964), 60
Classical studies, 77
Cocaine, 104
Cochran v. the Louisiana State Board of Education (1930), 95
"Cognitive dissonance," 104–105
Coleman, James S., 62, 65, 120
Coleman Report—*See Equality of Educational Opportunity*
Collective bargaining, 106

College involvement, 130–131
College of Teachers (Cincinnati), 43
Colonial America: literacy, 36; schooling in, 15–20; teachers, 107–108
Columbia University, 87
Common school, 20–22, 127; forerunners of, 18–20; patriotism and, 42–43; teachers and, 108; universal literacy and, 37; upward mobility and, 39
Community involvement, 131
Community service: in core curriculum, 11; internships, 131–132
Compulsory education, 47–49
Computers, 102–103, 113–114
Conflict in Education in a Democratic Society, The, 86
Constitution, U.S.: in curriculum, 42–43; federal powers, 24–25, 27
Copperman, Paul, 8–9
Corporate involvement, 130
Corruption, 83
Costs—*See Funding*
Covello, Leonard, 51
Creationism, 91–93
Cremin, Lawrence, 22, 32–33
Crime, in-school, 103–104
Criticism of public education, 33
Cultural literacy, 88
Curriculum, 73–99; basic education approach, 87–90; "cafeteria" style, 10; Committee of Ten proposal, 5; community service and, 11; controversies, 96–98; essentialist approach, 78–80; "good" education and, 74–75; "knowledge" and, 75–76; perennialist approach, 76–78; preparation for real world, 74; progressivist approach, 80–87, 98; religion in, 90–96; teachers and, 104

Dame schools, 15–16
Darrow, Clarence, 91
Darwin, Charles, 91
Declaration of Independence, 66
Democracy, 132; John Dewey on, 22; Thomas Jefferson on,

137

19, 36; progressivism and, 81; schools as embodiment, 44
Democracy and Education, 84–85
Department of Education, U.S., 27
Desegregation, 60–66; *Brown* decision and, 58–60; Civil Rights Act (1964) and, 60–61; Coleman Report and, 64–65; New York City, 64; World War II and, 58
Detroit, 64–65
Dewey, John, 22, 84–85, 106
Dictionaries, 37
Digest of Education Statistics, 104
Disabled, 70–71
Discipline: in early America, 16; increasing problem of, 103; as parental concern, 97; pupil achievement and, 120
Discrimination, 58, 60–61
Diversity, cultural and ethnic, 45, 51
Driver education, 130
Dropping-out, 124; rate of, 3; study on (1909), 6
Drug abuse, 97–98, 103, 104
Du Bois, W. E. B., 56

Early education, 128
Economic conditions, 32, 38–39, 45
Economic Opportunity Act (1964), 69
Educating Americans for the 21st Century (1983), 11
Education, U.S. Department of, 9
Education, U.S. Office of, 27
Educational Wastelands, 87
Education and Labor, U.S. Senate Committee on, 56–57
Education Commission of the States, 11
"Education for All Handicapped Children Act" (Public Law 94-142), 71
Educators, overstatement of school's benefits by, 4
Elementary and Secondary Education Act (1965), 60
Emancipation Proclamation, 53
Engle v. Vitale (1962), 96
English language: American English, 43–44; bilingual education, 67; immigrants, 37
Epperson v. Arkansas (1968), 93
Equality of Educational Opportunity (1966), 61–65

"Equal protection" clause, 53
Esquivel, Rita, 69
Essentialism, 78–80, 104–105
Everson v. the Board of Education (1947), 94, 95
Evolution, 91–93
Extracurricular activities, 44, 96

Family background, role of, 63
Federal government: bilingual education and, 67–69; desegregation and, 60–61; and disabled students, 70–71; funding by, 56–57; involvement of, 26–27; religious affairs and, 94–95; Sputnik and, 87
Federalism, 24
Feistritzer, C. Emily, 109
Fernandez, Joseph A., 125
Fifteenth Amendment (voting rights), 52, 55
Film, 113
Final Report (Committee on School Inquiry, 1911-1913), 6
Fine, Benjamin, 7
Finland, 129
First Amendment (freedom of expression), 21, 90–91, 93, 94
Flag, American, 42
Flesch, Rudolf, 7, 89
Foreign countries: American students compared, 9; length of school year, 128; statistics, 3–4
Foreign language instruction, 10, 112
Fortune (magazine), 37
Forum (journal), 82–83
Fourteenth Amendment (equal protection), 52–53, 93
Franklin, Benjamin, 18
Franklin, John Hope, 54
Freedmen's Bureau, 53
Froebel, Friedrich, 30
Fulbright, William, 57
Fundamentalism, 92–93
Funding, 7; attacks on progressivism and, 87; disparities in, 125–126; by federal government, 56–57; handicapped, 71; inequality and, 51–52; 1990 versus 1980, 127; school-choice and, 118–119; statistics, 24

Galbraith, John Kenneth, 105
Gifted children, 9, 128
Goodlad, John, 11, 33–34, 97–98
Grammar, 37
"Great books," 76–78

Greek (language), 17, 18
Greer, Colin, 49
Grover, Herbert J., 117
Guns, in-school, 3

Handicapped—*See Disabled*
Harris, Benjamin, 37
Harris, William Torrey, 35
Head Start program, 69–70, 128
Health, Education and Welfare, U.S. Department of, 61
Henry Eggers Middle School (Hammond, Indiana), 126
Herbart, Johann Friedrich, 30
Higher order intellectual skills, 10
Highland Park High School (Dallas, Texas), 125–126
High School: A Report on Secondary Education in America, 11
High schools: enrollment, 48–49; ladder system, 27–28; student concerns, 97–98
High/Scope Education Research Foundation, 70
History of public education: government involvement, 26–27; Massachusetts Bay Colony, 15, 17–18; mythical golden age of, 4–5; 19th and early 20th centuries, 5–6; teachers, 107–108; World War II to 1960s, 6–8
Holmes, William (1800–1873), 37
Home economics, 40
Homework, 120; foreign schools, 3–4
Horace's Compromise, 11–12
Hornbook, 16
Horne, Herman C., 80
Hungary, 129
Hutchins, Robert, 77, 86

Illiteracy, 8—*See also* Literacy; adults, 9; Colonial America, 36; early 20th century, 6; teenagers, 9; World War II, 6–7
Immigrants: bilingual education, 66–69; inequality in schools and, 50–51; schools and integration of, 37, 44, 45
Independent schools, 48
Inequality, 49, 50–52
Innumeracy, 8
Integration—*See Desegregation*
Intelligence quotient (IQ), 84
Intelligence testing, 84
Interior, U.S. Department of the, 27

Intermediate schools, 29
International Association for the Evaluation of Educational Achievement, 129
Internships, 131–132
Investment in education, 3
"Invisible hand," 114–115, 122
IQ—See Intelligence quotient

Jefferson, Thomas: common school, 18–19; First Amendment, 90; on literacy, 36; perennialism and, 78
Jim Crow laws, 55, 59
John James Audubon Elementary School (San Diego, California), 126–127
Johnson, Andrew, 27
Johnson, Lyndon B., 60, 64
Johnson, Samuel, 132
Junior high schools, 28–29

Kalamazoo (Michigan), 27–28
Kappan (journal), 33
Kindergarten, 28, 30
Knights of the White Camellia, 54
Knowledge, subjectivity of, 75–76
Ku Klux Klan, 54

Ladder system, 18, 27–29
Latin (language), 17, 18
Latin grammar school, 17
Lau v. Nichols (1974), 68
Library, school, 103
"Life adjustment education" programs, 85–86
Lincoln, Abraham, 53
Lincoln School (Columbia University Teachers College), 87
Literacy, 35–38—See also Illiteracy
Literary Hoax, The, 8–9
Louisiana, 55

Mainstreaming, 71
Making of a Teacher, The (1984), 109
Making the Grade (1983), 10–11
Mann, Horace, 20, 35, 38, 49, 50
Manual arts, 40–41
Marijuana, 104
Massachusetts: Bay Colony, 17–18; compulsory education, 47
Mass education, 20–21, 34–35
Mathematics, 10

McCollum v. the Board of Education (1948), 95
McGuffey Readers, 37
Memorization, 16
Metropolitan school districts (Detroit), 64–65
Michigan Supreme Court, 28
Middle Ages, 77
Milliken v. Bradley (1974), 65
Mississippi, 47
Moe, Terry M., 117–118
Morality, 21
Morgan, J. P., 82
Morrill Act (1862), 26
Muckrakers, 82
Multiculturalism, 69, 126
Myrdal, Gunnar, 58

National Association for the Advancement of Colored People (NAACP), 56, 117
National Association of Educational Progress, 36
National Association of Manufacturers, 41
National Center for Education Information, 105, 109–110
National Commission on Excellence in Education, The, 128
National Education Association (NEA), 5, 41, 56, 70, 106
National Science Board, 11
National service, 131–132
Nation at Risk, A (1983), 2–4, 9, 10, 12, 127–128
Native Americans, 22
Neighborhood schools, 64
New England Freedmen's Aid Society, 53
New England Primer, The, 37
New York City, 124–125, 129
New York City Board of Education, 64
New York State Board of Regents, 96
New York Times, The, 7, 8
Niche education, 121
Nixon, Richard M., 71
Non-academic aspects of schools, 15
Normal school, 108
Northwest Ordinance (1787), 26
Numeracy, 35–36

Office of Education, U.S., 62, 68
"Old Deluder Satan Act" (1647), 17–18
One-room schoolhouse, 16, 105
Oregon, 48

Padeia Proposal, 78
Parents: concerns, 97–98; involvement, 116, 126–127; rating by, 33–34
Parent-Teacher Association (PTA), 126
Parker, Francis W., 30–31
Parochial schools, 48
Patriotism, 21, 41–45
Pennsylvania, University of, 18
Perennialism, 76–78
Pestalozzi, Johann Heinrich, 30
Phi Delta Kappa, 33
Philosophy of education, 30–31
Phonics method, 89–90
Pierce v. The Society of Sisters of Jesus and Mary (1925), 48
Place Called School, A, 11, 33
Plato, 77
Plessy v. Ferguson (1896), 55
Politics, Markets, and America's Schools, 117–118
Pollock, Thomas Clark, 112
Poor children: common school, 21–22; inequality in education, 50–52; school-choice, 116–117
"Power sharing," 125
Prayer, school, 96
Pregnancy, teen, 3
Principals, 98, 121
Private schools, 100, 117
Progressive education, 80–87; attacks on, 86–89; legacy of, 98; reading and, 90; teacher role, 104–105
Progressive Education (journal), 98
Progressive Education Association, 98
Progressive Era, 82
Protestantism, 17
Psychology, progressivism and, 84
PTA—See Parent-Teacher Association
Public Law 94-142 (1975), 71

Racial Isolation in the Public Schools (1967), 64
Racial percentages, 61
Racial prejudice, 58
Racism, bilingual education and, 66
Railroads, segregation on, 55
Reader, 37
Reading, theories of teaching, 89–90
Reagan, Ronald, 68–69, 103–104
"Real world," preparing stu-

dents for, 74
Reconstruction (1865–1876), 53–54
Reform: nineteenth century, 20; parental involvement, 116
Rehabilitation Act (1973), 70–71
Religion: curriculum, 90–96; early American schools, 17
Remedial education, 10
Renaissance, 77
Restoration of Learning, The, 87
Rhode Island, 18
Ribicoff, Abraham, 59
Rice, Joseph Mayer, 82–83
Rochester (New York), 124
Rockefeller, John D., 82
Rockfish Gap Report (1819), 36
Russia, 40
Rutter, Michael, 119–120

Salaries, teacher, 7, 110, 125
Salinger, J. D., 103
SAT—*See Scholastic Aptitude Test*
Scholarships, 19
Scholastic Aptitude Test (SAT), 10
School and Society, 22
School board, 25
School day, length of, 102
School districts, 25–26
School Inquiry, Committee on, 6
Schools: atmosphere, 120; parents' right to choose, 114–119; recognizing good, 119–122; small, 129
School year, length of, 3, 102, 127–128
Schultz, Theodore W., 41
Science, 10
Scopes, John T., 91
Secondary Studies, Committee of Ten on (1984), 5
Security guards, 103
Segregation—*See also Desegregation*: Coleman Report and, 63–65; school-choice and, 116–117; "separate but equal" policy, 23, 55–56; World War II and, 58
"Separate but equal" doctrine, 23, 55–56
Service requirements, 131–132
Sesame Street, 112
Sex education, 103
Shanker, Albert, 1–2
Sherman, William Tecumseh, 54
Shop courses, 40

Silberman, Charles, 65
Singleton v. Jackson Municipal Separate School District (1970), 61
Sizer, Theodore, 11–12
Slavery, 53
Small schools, 129
Smith, Adam, 114, 119
Socialization, 81
Society, schools and, 101–104, 123–127
Socrates, 77
Socratic method, 78
Some Proposals Relating to the Education of Youth in Pennsylvania, 18
Southern states: late 19th and early 20th centuries, 54–56; Reconstruction, 53–54
Special education, 71
Sputnik, 7, 87
States: authority over education, 24–25; certification by, 109–111, 118; superintendent of schools, 25
Statistical Abstract of the United States, 24
Stowe, Calvin, 108
Stowe, Harriet Beecher, 108
Strikes, teacher, 106–107
Subject matter—*See Curriculum*
Suffrage, 19
Supreme Court, U.S.: bilingual education, 68; compulsory education, 48; creationism, 93; desegregation, 23, 59–61; federal authority and, 27; metropolitan school districts, 65; religion in schools, 94–96; "separate but equal" doctrine, 55

Talks on Pedagogics, 30–31
Taxation, 21, 38, 52
Teachers: changes affecting, 100; compromises by, 11–12; conflicting messages given to, 104–105; lack of power of, 105; patriotic role of, 42–43; preparation and certification, 107–110; salaries in 1940s, 7; satisfaction of, 110; shortages of, 110–111; strikes by, 106–107; students and parents on, 97; technology and, 112–114; unionization of, 105–107
Teaching: essentialist view of, 80; instruction in methods of, 109; perennialist view of, 78; reading, 89; Joseph M. Rice on,

83; television and, 112–113
Technology: absence of, 102; future of, 129–130; teaching and, 100, 112–114
Teenage pregnancy, 103
Television, 3, 112–113
Tennessee, 54, 91
Tenth Amendment (states' rights), 24
Testing, essentialist view of, 79
Test scores, 3
Texas, 125–126
Textbooks, 103
Thirteenth Amendment (slavery abolition), 52
Thurow, Lester, 128
Time for Results (1986), 115
Tocqueville, Alexis de, 35
Tuition: early America, 16–17
Twentieth-Century Fund, 10

Unions, 105–107
Universities, public, 26
University involvement, 130–131
Upchurch, Wilma, 57
Upward mobility, 39

Values: "good" education, 74–75; societal, 39, 47
Vanderbilt, Cornelius, 82
Video, 112–113
Virginia, 19
Vocational education, 40–41
Vouchers, 116–117

War of 1812, 42
Washington, Booker T., 56
Wealth of Nations, The, 114
Webster, Noah, 37, 43
"White flight," 65
Whitehead, Alfred North, 129
Whole word method, 89–90
Why Johnny Can't Read, 7, 89
Williams, Polly, 117
Wisconsin, 117
Wisdom, John Minor, 61
Women: teacher shortage and, 110–111
Woodward, Calvin M., 40
Work stoppages, 106
World Telegram and Sun, 8
World War II, 58

Yale University, 130

Zorach v. Clauson (1952), 95